Understanding
JOSEPH ROTH

Understanding Modern
European and Latin American
Literature

James Hardin, *Series Editor*

*volumes on*

Ingeborg Bachmann
Samuel Beckett
Thomas Bernhard
Johannes Bobrowski
Heinrich Böll
Italo Calvino
Albert Camus
Elias Canetti
Camilo José Cela
Céline
José Donoso
Friedrich Dürrenmatt
Rainer Werner Fassbinder
Max Frisch
Federico García Lorca
Gabriel García Márquez
Juan Goytisolo
Günter Grass
Gerhart Hauptmann

Christoph Hein
Hermann Hesse
Eugène Ionesco
Uwe Johnson
Milan Kundera
Primo Levi
Boris Pasternak
Octavio Paz
Luigi Pirandello
Graciliano Ramos
Erich Maria Remarque
Alain Robbe-Grillet
Joseph Roth
Jean-Paul Sartre
Claude Simon
Mario Vargas Llosa
Peter Weiss
Franz Werfel
Christa Wolf

# UNDERSTANDING

# JOSEPH
# ROTH

### SIDNEY ROSENFELD

UNIVERSITY OF SOUTH CAROLINA PRESS

UNIVERSITY OF SOUTH CAROLINA *BICENTENNIAL*

© 2001 University of South Carolina

Published in Columbia, South Carolina, by the
University of South Carolina Press

Manufactured in the United States of America

05   04   03   02   01      5   4   3   2   1

**Library of Congress Cataloging-in-Publication Data**

Rosenfeld, Sidney.
  Understanding Joseph Roth / Sidney Rosenfeld.
    p.  cm. — (Understanding modern European and Latin American literature)
  Includes bibliographical references and index.
  ISBN 1-57003-398-6 (alk. paper)
  1. Roth, Joseph, 1894–1939—Criticism and interpretation.  I. Title.  II. Series.
PT2635.O84 Z83   2001
833'.912—dc21                                                      00-011632

*For Stella and Natania*

# Contents

Editor's Preface    ix

Preface    xi

Abbreviations    xiii

Chronology    xv

Chapter 1    Introduction    1

Chapter 2    The Early Work, 1923–1924: Beginnings of a Career    16

Chapter 3    The Early Work, 1927–1929: New Objectivism and Its Limits    26

Chapter 4    The Pinnacle Years, 1930–1932: The Jewish and Austrian Themes    39

Chapter 5    The Exile Years, 1933–1937: The Novels of Guilt and Repentance    56

Chapter 6    The Exile Years, 1938–1939: Return to the Theme of Austria    74

Chapter 7    Riddles of a Torn Existence    87

Notes    99

Selected Bibliography    113

Index    121

# Editor's Preface

*Understanding Modern European and Latin American Literature* has been planned as a series of guides for undergraduate and graduate students and nonacademic readers. Like the volumes in its companion series *Understanding Contemporary American Literature,* these books provide introductions to the lives and writings of prominent modern authors and explicate their most important works.

Modern literature makes special demands, and this is particularly true of foreign literature, in which the reader must contend not only with unfamiliar, often arcane artistic conventions and philosophical concepts, but also with the handicap of reading the literature in translation. It is a truism that the nuances of one language can be rendered in another only imperfectly (and this problem is especially acute in fiction), but the fact that the works of European and Latin American writers are situated in a historical and cultural setting quite different from our own can be as great a hindrance to the understanding of these works as the linguistic barrier. For this reason the UMELL series emphasizes the sociological and historical background of the writers treated. The philosophical and cultural traditions peculiar to a given culture may be particularly important for an understanding of certain authors, and these are taken up in the introductory chapter and also in the discussion of those works to which this information is relevant. Beyond this, the books treat the specifically literary aspects of the author under discussion and attempt to explain the complexities of contemporary literature lucidly. The books are conceived as introductions to the authors covered, not as comprehensive analyses. They do not provide detailed summaries of plot because they are meant to be used in conjunction with the books they treat, not as a substitute for study of the original works. The purpose of the books is to provide information and judicious literary assessment of the major works in the most compact, readable form. It is our hope that the UMELL series will help increase knowledge and understanding of European and Latin American cultures and will serve to make the literature of those cultures more accessible.

J. H.

# Preface

Thirty-five years ago I completed my doctoral dissertation on Joseph Roth at the University of Illinois. I had come upon him by chance. While browsing in the library stacks one afternoon, the bright orange binding of a three-volume set caught my eye. It was the first edition of Roth's works, edited by his friend Hermann Kesten. I took the middle volume from the shelf. It began with the novel *Hiob,* and the very first lines engrossed me: "Many years ago there lived in Zuchnow a man named Mendel Singer. He was pious, God-fearing, and ordinary, an entirely everyday Jew. He practiced the simple occupation of a teacher. In his house, which was just a large kitchen, he taught the Bible to children." In Roth's children's teacher I recognized my grandfather. He, too, had been a *melamed* in tsarist Russia. In the social hierarchy of the small east European Jewish town, perhaps only the water carrier stood lower. Like Roth's Mendel Singer, my grandfather had also been impecunious (and remained so in America, to be exact, in the Jewish immigrant quarter of South Philadelphia where he settled in 1904). And the home in which my mother was raised for twenty years without him (since he left their Podolian village for America just weeks after her birth, and as a widower), likewise consisted of a single room. As I read more of Roth, the kinship with him grew closer, and in place of Karl Kraus, my burning interest at that time, I elected to write my doctoral thesis on him.

As personally moved as I had been, the thesis betrayed precious little of the intimacy I felt with Roth, not only with *Job* and the later "Russian" novels, but also with his Austrian works, above all *The Radetzky March.* My approach was utterly ahistorical, a formal study in the mode of the then-current interpretative school of Wolfgang Kayser and Emil Staiger. Only after Roth's collected letters appeared in 1970, and David Bronsen's groundbreaking biography in 1974, did I begin to read Roth with a heightened awareness of his person and his historical time and place. The chance to revisit his books with bright students at Oberlin College, and to write on him, also helped to broaden the horizon before which I now viewed him. Meanwhile, the secondary literature—dissertations, books, essays, articles, symposia proceedings—kept growing. The more I learned about the man and writer, the clearer it became that his early postwar commentators—

among them his friends Hermann Kesten and Irmgard Keun, and other, younger writers—had already recognized what was most essential to him and his work. Time had passed, but their characterizations had only gained in persuasiveness. Roth had truly been a writer "without a home on this earth" (H. Böll), a "wanderer in flight toward a tragic end" (O. Forst de Battaglia), a "Jew in search of a fatherland" (Bronsen). And without question he had been a loving, if not full, member of two communities, the east European Jewish and the Habsburg Austrian. And yes, he had also been a "Maskenspieler," a dissembler, as Kesten claimed, or, as Bronsen put it, a "mythomaniac." If I wished to describe my book with the help of a subtitle, I would have had to invent still another variation on one, or more than one, of these. For this is also how I have learned to see Joseph Roth, and what my book is about.

When I finished writing, I felt confident that I had gained new clarity on Roth and his work. But I must confess that again and again, in moments when I felt I had drawn closer to him, I saw him slip from my grasp. The enigmas and riddles that he presents in his unending search for a home remained for me as impenetrable as his gaze in the familiar photo of 1938, where iris and pupil merge in a dark pool. This caused me more than a little unease, but finally I accepted the fact that the enigmas and riddles are irresolvable. This recognition is essential if we wish to understand Joseph Roth's failures and appreciate his accomplishments.

# Abbreviations

Unless otherwise noted, citations of works by Joseph Roth will be of English translations. At first citation, a full entry will be provided in an endnote. Thereafter, quotations from Roth will be cited parenthetically in the text using abbreviations based on the English titles.

| | |
|---|---|
| *AC* | *Der Antichrist* (Antichrist) |
| BE | "Die Büste des Kaisers" (The Bust of the Emperor) |
| *BR* | *Briefe* (Letters; my translations) |
| *CM* | *Beichte eines Mörders* (Confession of a Murderer) |
| *ET* | *Die Kapuzinergruft* (The Emperor's Tomb) |
| *FE* | *Die Flucht ohne Ende* (Flight without End) |
| *HD* | *Die hundert Tage* (The Ballad of the Hundred Days) |
| *HS* | *Hotel Savoy* (Hotel Savoy) |
| *J* | *Hiob* (Job) |
| *LD* | *Die Legende vom Heiligen Trinker* (The Legend of the Holy Drinker) |
| *P* | *Perlefter* (Perlefter) |
| *R* | *Die Rebellion* (Rebellion) |
| *RL* | *Rechts und Links* (Right and Left) |
| *RM* | *Radetzkymarsch* (The Radetzky March) |
| *SP* | *Der stumme Prophet* (The Silent Prophet) |
| *SW* | *Das Spinnennetz* (The Spider's Web) |
| *T* | *Tarabas* (Tarabas) |
| *TN* | *Die Geschichte von der 1002. Nacht* (The Tale of the 1002nd Night) |
| *W* | *Werke* (Works; my translations) |
| *WM* | *Das falsche Gewicht* (Weights and Measures) |
| *ZF* | *Zipper und sein Vater* (Zipper and His Father) |

# Chronology

| | |
|---|---|
| **1894** | Moses Joseph Roth born on 2 September in Brody, Galicia (Austria) to Nochum Roth and Maria (Mirjam) Roth née Grübel. Father falls victim to insanity and is placed in care before Roth's birth; he never returns. Boy grows up as half-orphan with mother in grandfather's home. |
| **1901–1905** | Attends Baron Hirsch School of the Brody Jewish community. |
| **1905–1913** | Attends Royal-Imperial Crown-Prince Rudolf Gymnasium in Brody. |
| **1913–1914** | Spends one semester at Royal-Imperial University in Lemberg. Transfers to University of Vienna. |
| **1914–1916** | Studies German literature in Vienna. Publishes poems, stories, and essays in Vienna newspapers. |
| **1916** | Volunteers for military service in World War I. |
| **1917–1918** | Stationed in Galicia. Assigned to Army News Service. Publishes in Austrian newspapers. |
| **1919–1920** | Writes prolifically as staff member of Vienna daily *Der Neue Tag*. |
| **1920** | Moves to Berlin, where he writes for several papers. |
| **1922** | Marries Friederike Reichler (1900–1940), daughter of Galician-Jewish parents, in Vienna. |
| **1923** | Moves with Friederike from Berlin back to Vienna. Publishes in *Prager Tagblatt*. Newspaper publication of *Das Spinnennetz* (*The Spider's Web*, 1989) marks debut as novelist. Returns to Berlin, where he works as a correspondent for *Frankfurter Zeitung*. |
| **1924** | Publishes novels *Hotel Savoy* (*Hotel Savoy*, 1986) and *Die Rebellion* (*Rebellion*, 1999). |
| **1925** | Moves to Paris as feuilleton correspondent for *Frankfurter Zeitung*. Writes travel reports from southern France. Writes posthumously published series *Die weißen Städte*. |
| **1926** | Travels extensively in Soviet Union for *Frankfurter Zeitung*. Series "Reise in Rußland" begins appearing in fall. Becomes disillusioned with socialism. |

| | |
|---|---|
| **1927** | Publishes travel reports from Albania in *Frankfurter Zeitung*. Start of lifelong friendship with Austrian writer Stefan Zweig. Book-essay *Juden auf Wanderschaft* (*The Wandering Jews*, 2000) and *Die Flucht ohne Ende* (*Flight without End*, 1930) published. |
| **1928** | Friederike's emotional problems become acute. Roth's drinking increases. Extended travels during spring and summer in Poland. "Briefe aus Polen" appears in *Frankfurter Zeitung*. Writes travel reports from Italy in fall. *Zipper und sein Vater* (*Zipper and His Father*, 1989) published. |
| **1929** | Friederike's illness diagnosed as schizophrenia. Roth quits *Frankfurter Zeitung* to write for papers and journals in Munich and Berlin. Meets Andrea Manga Bell and begins a six-year liaison. *Rechts und Links* (*Right and Left*, 1992) published. Partial printing of posthumous novel *Der stumme Prophet* (*The Silent Prophet*, 1980). |
| **1930** | *Hiob* (*Job*, 1931) appears. Rejoins *Frankfurter Zeitung* as feuilletonist. Publishes *Panoptikum*, a selection of previously printed feuilletons. |
| **1932** | *Radetzkymarsch* (*The Radetzky March*, 1933) published. |
| **1933** | Leaves Berlin for Paris on 30 January. Beginning of permanent exile, marked by an unsteady existence in hotels (Hôtel Foyot, later Hôtel de la Poste). Becomes regular contributor to exile papers and journals (*Das Neue Tage-Buch*). Novella *Stationschef Fallmerayer* (*Fallmerayer the Stationmaster*, 1986) appears in anthology edited by H. Kesten. |
| **1934** | Writes further for exile and French papers and journals. *Der Antichrist* (*Antichrist*, 1935) and *Tarabas* (*Tarabas*, 1934) published. Short stories appear in French translation (including "Die Büste des Kaisers" ["The Bust of the Emperor," 1938]). |
| **1935** | Writes until 1938 for Austrian journal *Der Christliche Ständestaat*. *Die Hundert Tage* (*The Ballad of the Hundred Days*, 1936). |
| **1936** | Ends liaison with Andrea Manga Bell. Forms new relationship with German émigré writer Irmgard Keun (1905–1982). *Beichte eines Mörders* (*Confession of a Murderer*, 1938) published. |
| **1937** | Conducts a two-month lecture tour in Poland. *Das falsche Gewicht* (*Weights and Measures*, 1982) published. |
| **1938** | Last visit to Vienna. Represents Austrian monarchists in attempt to prevent Nazi Anschluss. *Die Kapuzinergruft* (*The Emperor's Tomb*, 1985) published. |

**1939**    Dies 27 May of delirium tremens and pneumonia in Hôpital
Necker (Paris). *Die Geschichte von der 1002. Nacht* (*The Tale of
the 1002nd Night,* 1998) published. The story "Die Legende vom
heiligen Trinker" appears posthumously (The Legend of the Holy
Drinker, 1989).

**1940**    Friederike is murdered by the Nazis in an Austrian psychiatric
hospital

# Understanding
## JOSEPH ROTH

# CHAPTER 1

# Introduction

By 30 January 1933, the day Adolf Hitler came to power in Germany, the Austrian-born writer Joseph Roth had published seven novels as well as two books of essays and feuilletons and was one of the most highly reputed journalists of his time. His two most recent novels, *Hiob* (Job) in 1930 and *Radetzkymarsch* (The Radetzky March) in 1932, had earned him his first pronounced successes and positioned him for still greater prominence. Nonetheless, he knew well that he was subject to the same mortal threat that the Nazis and their racial doctrine leveled at every other Jew within Germany. Only hours before Hitler was named Reich chancellor, Roth packed his sparse belongings, quit Berlin by train, and headed for Paris to begin a life in exile. In the six years that followed he lived precariously, traveling intermittently between various cities in southern France, Switzerland, Belgium, and Holland. At times he suspended his travels for a longer stay. In 1934 he shared a house for almost a year on the French Riviera (in Nice) with fellow exiles, among them his friend and later editor, Hermann Kesten, and the novelist Heinrich Mann. There he met frequently with numerous other well-known German and Austrian exile writers who lived nearby. In 1936 he spent some three months in Ostende, again in the company of Kesten and also the writers Stefan Zweig, Ernst Toller, and Egon Erwin Kisch, all of whom were soon to seek safe haven in the Americas.

Until Austria's annexation by Nazi Germany in 1938, Roth also traveled to Vienna and Salzburg for visits with family and friends and for literary reasons. In 1937, at the invitation of the Polish P.E.N. Club, he spent two trying months on a lecture tour of several cities in Poland in an effort to bolster his chronically scant means. In the main, however, his domicile was a simple Paris hotel room. Helped by a circle of friends and advances from his Dutch publishers (however uncertain), he habitually wrote at a bistro or café table—always by hand and in a tiny, almost calligraphic script that, like his dapper dress, seemed to belie his despair and ebbing health. As the pages accumulated before him—he could write for hours on end with full concentration—so did the empty liquor glasses at his elbow. On 27 May 1939, ruined by drink, he died in Paris at the age of forty-four. His gravestone at Thiais Cemetery outside the city bears the inscription: ECRIVAIN AUTRICHIEN / MORT A PARIS EN EXIL. In 1939, on the eve of the Second World War, the epithet "Austrian Writer" for Joseph Roth, the outcast Jew and relentless foe of Nazism, could be regarded as a declaration of allegiance to a country that had ceased to exist and, however faint, a cry of defiance to its enemies.

Less than a half-year after Roth's flight from Germany, in May 1933, his books, along with those by scores of other proscribed writers, were publicly burned by Nazi-organized student mobs. Although at this time Roth could have still arranged to have his work appear in the Third Reich, he vehemently refused any type of collaboration with publishers there, and he castigated in the strongest terms those writers who did compromise themselves. Thus, to the generation of readers in Germany and his native Austria who had yet to come of age when the twelve years of the Nazi dictatorship began, he was an unknown writer, and after the defeat of the Third Reich he remained virtually forgotten for over ten years. Before the mid-1960s his name was missing altogether from the official lists of recommended reading for German public schools.[1] Similarly, in a standard reference work intended for use at the university level, Heinz Otto Burger's *Annalen der deutschen Literatur* (1952), there is no mention of Roth whatsoever; even as late as 1955, his name failed to appear in the sixth edition of Fritz Martini's *Deutsche Literaturgeschichte,* an affordable literary history read by almost all German university students. To be sure, until well into the 1950s, this was a fate Roth and his work shared with many German exile writers. In both East and West Germany there was either scant interest in rediscovering more than a few of those authors who had fled Nazi Germany or there was actual resistance to doing so. From the start, the cultural politics of the occupying forces, above all the Americans and the Soviets, strongly influenced these developments—with each side favoring those writers they deemed useful to their ends and shunning all others.

Altogether, the political climate—restorative in West Germany, rigidly dogmatic in socialist East Germany—a generally inimical stance by those writers who had remained in the Third Reich, and disinterest on the part of both publishers and academic scholars worked against mending the cultural rupture.[2] Two small printings in Holland, one in 1948 of the novel *Job,* which nearly twenty years earlier had marked Roth's breakthrough, and another two years later of his best-known work, *The Radetzky March,* were unable to rescue their author from obscurity. Aside from these hardly noticed efforts, the earliest postwar attempt to restore Roth's legacy was undertaken in 1949, when a volume of appreciative essays and personal recollections, all from the circle of the writer's intimate friends, commemorated his life and work.[3] Not until 1956, however, when Hermann Kesten edited and introduced *Werke in drei Bänden,* a three-volume edition of Roth's works, was the way paved for his discovery by new readers.[4]

A more modest yet significant marker of Roth's posthumous return from exile was the appearance in 1964 of *Romane, Erzählungen, Aufsätze,* a one-volume selection of novels, tales, and essays.[5] Thanks to its low cost, this book made a representative sampling of Roth's works accessible to a broader audience than did the *Werke.* It was especially noteworthy, moreover, because it included the original German version of a story, "Die Büste des Kaisers" (1934; The Bust of the Emperor), which in the 1956 *Werke* had appeared in French translation as "Le Buste de l'Empereur." In itself, this recourse to and subsequent rejection of a surrogate version is emblematic of the history of Roth's reemergence in Germany. Amid the urgencies of exile and the German occupation of France and its neighboring countries, Roth's manuscripts and letters were surreptitiously stored by friends or their fate was left more or less to chance. Through today, some of these materials remain lost, while still others have turned up unforeseen in libraries, archives, and private dwellings on two continents. By the time the newly expanded edition of the *Werke* was published between 1975 and 1976,[6] two more novels by Roth, a body of political articles from the twenties, and an extensive correspondence had been unearthed. The story "The Bust of the Emperor," as it turned out, had first been published in French translation in 1934, but the original German version had soon followed it in Paris as a serial in the German-language newspaper *Pariser Tageszeitung* from 28 July to 1 August 1935. Roth's editor, Kesten, it seems, was unaware either that the German version had ever been printed or that it still existed.

While "The Bust of the Emperor" appears to have been little more than an occasional piece intended to alleviate Roth's financial distress, its theme lies at the very heart of the author's work. In twenty pages it relates the story of the Austrian nobleman Count Franz Xaver Morstin, who is at the time of narration a retired army officer. Roth introduces the count as the scion of an old Polish family that had emigrated to Poland from Italy in the sixteenth century and founded an estate in the village of Lopatyny, which before World War I lay in the Austrian crownland of Galicia. Echoing what the poet Hugo von Hofmannsthal idealized as the Austrian Idea in a historical-political essay of 1917,[7] Roth describes Morstin in terms of his own lofty and ardently cherished understanding of Austrianism: "He thought of himself neither as a Polish aristocrat nor as an aristocrat of Italian origin. No: like so many of his peers in the former Crown Lands of the Austro-Hungarian monarchy, he was one of the noblest and purest sort of Austrian, plain and simple. That is, a man above nationality, and therefore of true nobility. Had anyone asked him, for example—but to whom would such a senseless question have occurred?—to which "nationality" or race he belonged, the Count would have felt rather bewildered, baffled even, by his questioner, and probably bored and somewhat indignant."[8]

This description—in its empathetic mode typical for Roth—conveys in a nutshell the theme of the tale that follows. The essence of Habsburg Austria, Roth tells us, was an all-embracing supranationality, intended to bind together the diverse peoples of the empire through a common ethos. As Count Morstin himself later epitomizes his homeland, Austria was "a great mansion with many doors and chambers, for every condition of men" (BE 183). Conversely, nationalism, indeed the very idea of a nation-state, was foreign to those Habsburg subjects who, like Morstin, lived their lives in natural and, as the biblical reference suggests, devout allegiance to the monarchy.[9] Like the count, who after 1918 found himself spiritually homeless, they, too, felt they had lost their place in the world when the monarchy was undermined by the movements of its peoples toward independent nation-states. In tension with national particularism, it is this historical phenomenon of Habsburg universality that, in idealized form, inspired the Austrian novels on which Roth's fame rests, above all his masterpiece, *The Radetzky March,* and its less imposing sequel, *Die Kapuzinergruft* (1938; *The Emperor's Tomb*).

Inseparable from the sustaining Austrian ideal of supranationality that Morstin represents was—for Roth personally, but historically as well—the centuries-old diaspora condition of Jewish homelessness. Within Habsburg Austria, the two were joined in a unique symbiotic relationship. Together, Jewish homelessness and Austrian universality in its period of decline constitute the thematic core of Roth's entire novelistic work. They also provide the key to understanding the enigmatic turns of Roth's life, from his youth in Galician Brody and his literary beginnings in Vienna and Berlin, to his latter years in French exile as a cultural conservative and monarchist.

Like Count Morstin of the story, Joseph Roth was a native of eastern Galicia. He was born on 2 September 1894 in the multiethnic town of Brody as the first and only child of Orthodox Jewish parents.[10] In wending his way from Brody to the west and a writer's career, first in the imperial city of Vienna and later in Weimar Berlin, Roth purposefully shed, or strived to shed, the characteristics that marked him not only as an *Ostjude,* an east European Jew, but as an *Ostjude* from Galicia, the most backward and disparaged of the Austrian crown provinces. The many false biographical claims, personal affectations, and subterfuges that early and later witnesses describe as peculiar to Roth's personality can be attributed to what he perceived to be the onus of his Galician-Jewish origins. This prime circumstance likewise found a variety of thematic and atmospheric expressions in his fictional, essayistic, and journalistic work. Once having overcome his early shame, again and again in his writings he returned to the town and region of his birth and upbringing with affection and often unmistakable pride.

Roth's long-time friend Kesten aptly characterized him as a *Maskenspieler,* a dissembler or player of divers roles. Roth's masquerade, or game of identity, began in prewar Vienna, when the fledgling university student assumed the demeanor of a dandy, complete with monocle, in an effort to disguise his humble Galician beginnings. In Vienna, too, he affected the melody and cadences of Viennese speech in order to mute his pronounced Galician accent. Similarly, on entering army service in 1916, he dropped his encumbering first name of Moses; later he claimed as his birthplace not Brody itself, but the immediate neighborhood of his family's home, Szwaby, calling it—with a hint of German cultural superiority—"Schwabendorf."[11] By turns he named as his natural father a Polish count, an Austrian railway official, an army officer, a Viennese munitions manufacturer, and still other figures—anything other than the plain Galician Jew Nochum Roth who succumbed to madness before his son's birth, never to be seen again in the circle of his family. It was likewise part of this *Maskenspiel* when the former infantry private Roth boasted of a wartime lieutenant's rank and wore narrow-cut trousers to suggest the uniform of an Austrian cavalry officer. Similarly, during his exile years in Paris after 1933, Roth strained the credulity of friends and benefactors with declarations of Catholic piety, while at the same time proudly, and paradoxically, claiming the identity of a genuine *Ostjude.*

The narrator of *The Radetzky March,* Roth's generational novel on the demise of Habsburg Austria, states that the dwellers of the Austrian borderlands felt the coming of upheaval long before it was perceived in the capital city of Vienna, "not only because they were used to sensing future things but also because they could see the omens of doom every day with their own eyes."[12] Here, Roth was speaking as someone from their own midst. He himself had been born into the climate of disquietude and ferment that heralded the breakup of the monarchy in the wake of the First World War. His native Galicia, in which the greatest part of the novel is set, was a crucible of the national disputes that eventually tore apart the multithreaded fabric of Imperial Austria. In his birthplace, Brody, the question of national or ethnic identity was hardly so incomprehensible or senseless as it appeared to Count Morstin of "The Bust of the Emperor." Rather, this question defined the lives of the town's inhabitants as well as the historical and political atmosphere of the epoch.

In Galicia, as elsewhere within the vast Habsburg realm, the language of the home, the naming of a child, and the choice of a school were matters fraught with practical consequences not only for the everyday lives of individuals but also for the very existence of national communities and for Austria itself. Each decision of this kind declared a family's loyalty to—or break from—a national or group identity. As a pupil at Baron Hirsch School, the elementary school maintained by the Jewish community of Brody, and then at Crown-Prince Rudolf Gymnasium, Moses Joseph Roth was primarily instructed in three languages: German, Polish, and, in religion class, Hebrew. Yet another language of instruction at the gymnasium was Ukrainian. The list of forty-four graduating pupils of Roth's class shows that twelve were Roman Catholic (and thus Polish), fourteen were Greek Catholic (i.e., Ukrainian), and seventeen were Jewish. Almost without exception, these Jewish students bore traditional Hebrew-Yiddish first names; for the majority of them, their family language was Yiddish.[13] On all sides, then, in the daily life of the town, Roth heard Yiddish, Polish, and Ukrainian.

In Roth's own family Yiddish was still understood, but neither his mother nor uncles spoke the language; they had already been assimilated to speak German. Yet Roth acquired a familiarity with Yiddish that went beyond rudimentary usage and this enabled him to converse in it, even if faultily.[14] In his later, exile years, he at times turned to a Yiddish phrase as if to seek comfort in something familiar from a long-buried past. The German émigré writer Irmgard Keun (1910–1982), Roth's steady companion in the mid-1930s, illustrates Roth's attachment to the language and the people who spoke it in her description of their 1937 trip to Poland. In Lemberg, she reported, Roth took her to visit an indigent Jewish family in a cellar dwelling, where "he sat down at the table and spoke Yiddish with them, in such a way that one could feel his love for humanity and that made me love him."[15]

At the time of Roth's birth, the Jews of Brody comprised some two-thirds of the town's 17,500 inhabitants. Over the course of the nineteenth century they had increasingly found themselves caught between the Poles and Ruthenians (as the Ukrainians of Old Austria were termed) in the struggle between these two groups for political and cultural hegemony—a struggle in which the Poles predominated. It typifies this clash of national wills and its implications for the Jews that Roth's revered German instructor at gymnasium, Max Landau, espoused the cause of Polish nationalism and saw Jewish assimilation to Polish culture as the path to the future in Galicia. Indeed, shortly after Roth's graduation in 1913, the official language of instruction at Crown-Prince Rudolf Gymnasium became Polish, and following World War I Brody was incorporated into Poland. For his part, however, Roth rejected the Polish option, as well as the Jewish national movement, of which Zionism was to become the most effective expression. He decided early to assimilate as an Austrian of German culture and to become a German writer.

Robert Musil (1880–1942) defines the character of this dual monarchy with consummate wit and irony in the chapter titled "Die große Sitzung" (The Great Session) in book one of his giant, uncompleted novel on Old Austria, *Der Mann ohne Eigenschaften* (1930–1943; The Man without Qualities). Musil ingeniously illuminates the existential quandary with which untold Habsburg subjects were faced. Austria itself, Musil explains, had no true name, at least not one suitable to everyday purposes. Rather—like the United States of America—it had a conglomerate, but decidedly less wieldy, designation intended to bridge what were insuperable national differences. In the same way, Musil suggests, Austrian identity itself had no homeland:

> [The] sense of the Austro-Hungarian state was so oddly put together that it must seem almost hopeless to explain it to anyone who has not experienced it himself. It did not consist of an Austrian part and a Hungarian part that, as one might expect, complemented each other, but of a whole and a part; that is, of a Hungarian and an Austro-Hungarian sense of statehood, the latter to be found in Austria, which in a sense left the Austrian sense of statehood with no country of its own. The Austrian existed only in Hungary, and there as an object of dislike; at home he called himself a national of the kingdoms and lands of the Austro-Hungarian monarchy as represented in the Imperial Council, meaning that he was an Austrian plus a Hungarian minus that Hungarian; and he did this not with enthusiasm but only for the sake of a concept that was repugnant to him, because he could bear the Hungarians as little as they could bear him, which added still another complication to the whole combination. This led many people to simply call themselves Czechs, Poles, Slovenes, or Germans.[16]

The one conspicuous exception to this ethnic-national "solution" to the problem of Austrian identity was the Jews. For them, the confluence of Jewish religious-ethnic and Austrian-imperial allegiance could exist without conflict. At the same time, however, they were the most uncertain and insecure representatives of such a merged identity. Alone among the peoples of the monarchy, they were unable to claim for themselves a historical national homeland within Austria or within Europe altogether. Although they were concentrated most densely in Galicia, they also lived scattered in greater or lesser numbers among all the peoples of the Habsburg realm. Until the period of their emancipation and the beginning of their acculturation during the German Enlightenment, they were regarded by their host peoples as an alien nation, and they also continued to see themselves as a distinct people in postbiblical exile. Even as they achieved civic equality they remained a foreign, though familiar, community amid the native populations. Little wonder, then, that in an epoch of intensifying nationalism in the Austrian lands, the Jews, more than all others, readily embraced the notion (however problematic) of an overarching, supranational Austrian identity and revered Emperor Franz Joseph as a protective, benevolent father. Another Old Austrian of Roth's generation, writer Jakob Klein-Haparash (1897–1970), who was born in Czernowitz in the crownland of Bukovina, reminisced in 1966 about this Jewish allegiance to Austria: "In Czernowitz, that farthest corner of the Habsburg monarchy, the Jews were the most loyal Austrian patriots. For my grandfathers, the Emperor came right after God, or better: They had two Gods, the great, inscrutable Jewish God and the 'good Franz Joseph.'"[17]

To become an Austrian, however, meant to assimilate in language, education, and custom to German culture as the historically bequeathed and politically fostered culture of Habsburg Austria. As did their brethren in Germany, and indeed wherever the European Enlightenment freed them from the fetters of a lesser, foreign status, the Jews of Austria pursued their assimilation with unparalleled ardor. By the turn of the twentieth century, the results were even more dramatic than in the neighboring German Reich. Concentrated in the larger cities of the monarchy, most notably in Vienna, Prague, and Budapest, the Jews of Austria attained not only economic power, but also a cultural preeminence far greater than they themselves would have dared to dream of but a few generations earlier. That their embrace of Germanness brought them at the same time into sharpened conflict with the ethnic populations among whom they lived—above all, Poles, Czechs, and Hungarians, but also the Germans of Austria themselves—was the reverse side of the coin.

Thus, Joseph Roth, at age nineteen, spent only one semester at the Imperial-Royal University of Lemberg (where he had enrolled in 1913) before moving on to study in Vienna. More fervidly than elsewhere in Galicia, the political and cultural strivings of Ruthenian/Ukrainian and Polish nationalism were played out in Lemberg, which—symptomatic of its history—changed names three times in the twentieth century: after World War I, Austrian Lemberg became Polish Lwów, then, in 1939, Russian Lvov, and finally, with the collapse of the Soviet Union in 1991, Ukrainian Lviv. Antagonism between the politically predominant Poles and the Ruthenians, who were reawakening to their own national identity, manifested themselves particularly vigorously in this city.[18] During the Polish-Ukrainian war of 1918–1919 for control of eastern Galicia, the "Lemberg Pogrom" in November 1918 cost some 340 innocent lives, the great majority of them Ukrainians, but also many Jews.[19] This long-seething climate of volatility could only have been deeply alienating for someone like Roth, whose religious-ethnic heritage stamped him as an outsider to both of the contending national groups. Thus, he quickly abandoned Lemberg for study in Vienna.

"A Christian in my courtyard is a rarity," the young student observed in a letter to his cousin Paula Grübel in 1916 (*BR* 33). He was writing from Vienna's Brigittenau district, which, together with the old ghetto of Leopoldstadt where he had lived during his first two years in Vienna, housed the largest part of the city's 200,000 Jews. In Brigittenau the vast majority of these Jews, like Roth himself, hailed from Galicia. In 1915, their numbers were further swelled by a flood of war refugees from the east, they too preponderantly from Galicia. Although Roth had set out firmly on the path to assimilation, his new environs inevitably called to mind the Jewish atmosphere of Brody that he had supposedly left behind. Later he was to write in his essay *Juden auf Wanderschaft* (1927; *The Wandering Jews*): "It is terribly hard to be an *Ostjude;* there is no harder lot than that of an *Ostjude* new to Vienna" (*W* 3:324).

The university student Roth was more privileged than the Jewish artisans, peddlers, and small shopkeepers who inhabited the tenements of Leopoldstadt and Brigittenau, but he recognized, and was potentially exposed to, the everyday social, religious, and racial prejudices that burdened their lives. His decision to study German literature, enshrined since early Romanticism as the treasure store of the German national heritage, linked him as could no other pursuit with the cultural world to which he aspired. Yet his Galician-Jewish background marked him as an outsider. Scanning the political map of Vienna, he described the problem of the Jews as outsiders that since the decline of nineteenth-century liberalism had grown more critical for all Jews in Austria, but especially for his fellow Jews from the east: "For the Christian Socials they are Jews. For the German Nationals they are Semites. For the Social Democrats they are unproductive elements" (*W* 3:331). Just two decades earlier, in 1897, Karl Lueger had become mayor of Vienna on a stridently anti-Semitic platform, and, beloved by the masses, he held this office until his death in 1910. Once elected, to be sure, the always pragmatic Lueger showed that his bite was less vicious than his constant booming bark, but the enmity toward Jews that he nourished among his supporters of artisans, small traders, and householders in Vienna's outlying districts remained virulent and helped prepare the way for Hitler—who later said in *Mein Kampf* that his five years in Vienna between 1906 and 1911 had permanently molded his racist and political views.

It was precisely the Jewish predicament Roth described, of being a rejected or, worse still, hated outsider, which had given impetus to political Zionism under the leadership of the Viennese journalist and playwright Theodor Herzl at the end of the previous century. In 1896, two years after Roth's birth, Herzl published his Zionist tract *Der Judenstaat* (The Jewish State), and a year later, under his presidency, the first World Zionist Congress was convened in Basel.

In light of the existential question of national belonging, Roth's *Maskenspiel* becomes comprehensible as the acting out of a new Viennese identity, even to the point of unwitting self-parody. It was the attempt of an *Ostjude* from Galicia to gain entrance to the world of a prewar Vienna that glittered beyond the dreary courtyards of Leopoldstadt and Brigittenau. Likewise, the voluntary enlistment of the convinced pacifist Roth for army service in World War I marked still another determined step toward assimilation.

When Roth returned from the war in mid-December 1918, the Habsburgs had been deposed and their far-flung empire of some fifty million inhabitants was reduced to the shrunken, German-speaking entity that became the First Austrian Republic. Its capital, Vienna, just yesterday the political, economic, and cultural hub of the monarchy, was cut off from the once seemingly inexhaustible reservoir of material and human resources that the crownlands had supplied it. Now home to nearly a third of the country's 6,500,000 population, the city seemed greatly oversized for its new role. In Austria's postwar climate of financial ruin, destitution, hunger, and political uncertainty, Roth was compelled to abandon his earlier university studies and, like all others, secure his personal livelihood. The prewar student and aspiring writer thus began his career as a journalist in Vienna, where he published within a single year over one hundred articles, mainly of local interest. When the newspaper he wrote for, *Der Neue Tag,* folded in 1920, Roth moved to Berlin, a city whose cultural receptivity and general openness to progressive trends had long beckoned to writers from Austria. Although inflation and political instability in the Weimar Republic were rampant, career opportunities for a writer were greater in Berlin than Vienna.

Shortly after this move, in 1922, Roth concluded what had been a stormy courtship in Vienna by marrying Friederike Reichler, the delicate, lovely, and intellectually unassuming daughter of simple Galician-Jewish parents. Following their nuptials, which took place in a Leopoldstadt synagogue, Roth and Friederike spent the next several years in Berlin (except for an interlude in Vienna in 1923). Living with his young Viennese bride in a rented apartment, for the first and only time in his life Roth approximated a domestic existence.

During this period, Roth distinguished himself as a topflight journalist, joining the prestigious *Frankfurter Zeitung* in 1923 as a regular staff member. Founded in 1856 by the democratic politician Leopold Sonnemann (1831–1909), the paper maintained its liberal, independent stance even during the Weimar Republic. Among its many well-known contributors were the authors Siegfried

Kracauer, Walter Benjamin, René Schickele, and Friedrich Sieburg. As a prized coworker, Roth was assigned to Paris in the spring of 1925, first as the paper's feuilleton correspondent, then as a foreign correspondent, a position that sent him traveling throughout Europe, including an extended trip through the Soviet Union in 1926 that resulted in a series of seventeen articles published as "Reise in Ruß-land" (Russian Journey). This latter experience in particular proved to be a major turning point in his political development. His socialist leanings, which had always been more a matter of human sympathy with the disadvantaged and exploited than one of practical engagement, were now dissipated. To Bernard von Brentano, his friend and colleague at the *Frankfurter Zeitung,* he wrote from Odessa: "By no means is the problem here political, but rather cultural, spiritual, religious, metaphysical" (*BR* 95). After four months, Roth returned from Russia convinced that the Great Revolution had betrayed its humanitarian ideals and that its gains were consumed by a new small-minded bourgeois materialism inspired by America.

This same period also saw the beginning of Roth's career as a novelist. Between the years 1923 and 1929, which mark the first phase of his literary development, Roth published six novels. The first of them, *Das Spinnennetz* (The Spider's Web), was initially printed as a newspaper serial in 1923, as was his next, *Hotel Savoy,* which appeared in the *Frankfurter Zeitung* in February and March of 1924. Later that same year, the novel was republished in book form in Berlin, and while it was actually Roth's second novel, it was generally viewed as his debut book until *The Spider's Web* was posthumously rediscovered. Although a second, illustrated edition of *Hotel Savoy* appeared in 1925, Roth complained that it had achieved far greater success in Russia than it had in Germany. Claiming that the novel had been translated four times into Russian, Roth asked, humorously but clearly also with chagrin, in a letter to a journalist colleague, but addressed as much to himself: "Am I a German writer?" (*BR* 48). The question was at least as old as Heinrich Heine. A century earlier, the Jewish Heine had confidently proclaimed in his *Buch der Lieder,* "I am a German poet / Renowned in German lands," while still knowing he was regarded as an outsider to Germandom and being wary about reviews mentioning his Jewishness. Many others after Heine—among them the popular author of village stories Berthold Auerbach (1812–1882) and, most poignantly of all, the novelist Jakob Wassermann (1873–1934)—came to know the pain of rejection and despaired over it. The literary historian Adolf Bartels (1862–1945), in fact, had made a career of tracing Jewish origins and denouncing as un-German any writer possessed of them; in 1933 Bartels's obsession became the norm.

At the outset of Roth's literary career, the question "Am I a German writer?"

11

perhaps only reveals the personal insecurity that the young author, bent on assimilation, had brought with him from Brody to the west. But once the Nazis assumed power, the same question, now forced on every Jewish writer, lost all possible meaning. A Jew might write in the German language, but by a decree that was translated into grim reality, he or she was not, nor could be, a German writer. And perhaps even in 1924 it was above all Roth's insecurity as a Jew that underlay his self-doubt. To the end, the lack of homeground beneath his feet as a German writer was to vex his existence and, with equal intensity, inspire his work. Like all writers, he, too, had to contend with the vagaries of the literary marketplace, but it surely would have been unthinkable for such writers as Thomas Mann or Bertolt Brecht to doubt their own legitimacy as German authors. Their right to it was unassailable. Even after Mann was divested of his citizenship in 1936 on the order of Hitler and his writings were proscribed during the Third Reich, his identity as a German remained beyond dispute; and, if after 1945 his hometown of Lübeck was slow to honor him as a native son, this had far more to do with lingering bourgeois narrow-mindedness than with any view of the writer or his books as un-German. Roth, however, had made his way to Vienna and then to Berlin as an outsider to Germanness, and, despite his later successes, he remained an outsider. After World War I, in fact, as a native of Galicia he was designated a Polish citizen and was compelled to apply for renaturalization as an Austrian; and, though he sometimes spoke in the plural of "We Germans," he never became a citizen of Germany.

Almost a decade before his books were consumed in the Nazi book burnings—like those of the many who were declared alien to the German race—the question of his belonging burdened him. The futile search for a *Heimat,* for rootedness in a national and cultural identity, was the personal experience that shaped Roth's entire life. Just as decisively, it defined his literary work—at times as an undercurrent, but in the works for which he is most notably remembered, above all the Austrian novels, as a surging inspirational source. Roth's quest for a deeper, more sustaining identity than the citizenship to which his Austrian passport attested led later commentators to epitomize him as "[a] wanderer in flight toward a tragic end," as "[a] Jew in search of a fatherland," and as a writer "in flight before the void."[20] This quest determined his most typical themes and gave rise to the specific Slavic-Jewish melancholy that lent color and tone to his narratives. More than any other component of his fictional work, Roth's masterful portrayals of homelessness and the search for home explain the profound appeal that has gained him an international readership beyond the German-language countries.

At a time when countless others, including writers and intellectuals, were still deluding themselves with the hope that, once in power, the Nazis would be moved toward moderation, Roth rejected such illusions. In political articles for the several socialist and liberal-left journals to which he regularly contributed and, somewhat later, for the *Frankfurter Zeitung,* he warned against the bloody threat that National-Socialism posed to the Weimar Republic. His 1922 series of nine articles for the *Berliner Abend-Zeitung* on the Rathenau murder trial underscores strikingly with what keen foresight Roth anticipated the German catastrophe under Hitler.[21] Although in 1933 Roth could have continued writing for the *Frankfurter Zeitung,* he refused the paper's offer as part of his steadfast opposition to the Third Reich. Above all, he regarded his stance as a moral and political one, but anti-Semitism, which would soon be legalized by the Nuremberg Laws of May 1935, necessarily added a strong personal dimension to it.

Only a short time before Hitler's ascent to power, the two works that mark the height of Roth's literary career, *Job* and *The Radetzky March,* had gained him acclaim as a major German novelist. Literally overnight Roth lost his German publishers as well as his readers, and, together with them, his livelihood in Germany. A year later, in 1934, well before the annexation of Austria by Nazi Germany on 14 March 1938, he discovered that he had also lost his sources of income in his native land, where he was ignored by the newspapers and editorial offices. From this point forward, he wrote for émigré journals in France and published his books with émigré presses in Holland. Despite ever-sparser publisher's advances and his own incessant drinking (especially problematic during his later exile years), Roth survived and somehow kept writing. The travails of these years are documented in the often desperate letters Roth assiduously penned to his publishers and friends, as he felt himself buffeted ever more relentlessly by misfortune. To his close friend and benefactor, Austrian author Stefan Zweig, Roth wrote in 1935 that alcohol "is shortening my life, that is true, but it is also preventing my *immediate* death" (*BR* 436).

Roth had embodied the Austrian theme for the first time in *The Radetzky March.* In the narrative works that followed, most notably the novel *Das falsche Gewicht* (1937; Weights and Measures), he incorporated Austrian motifs, but as a constitutive theme Austria reemerged only six years later in the novels *Die Kapuzinergruft* (1938; The Emperor's Tomb ) and *Die Geschichte von der 1002. Nacht* (1939; The Tale of the 1002nd Night). Throughout this entire period, however, Roth's nostalgic identification with Austria's imperial past and his fear for Austria's future fate figured prominently in his journalistic work. Stripped by Hitler's racial laws of his sense of German identity, which he defined in a cultural sense, but for a time also in a more concrete, ethnic one,[22] Roth fiercely committed himself to the political battle against the Third Reich and to the defense of Austrian independence. Although some of his notions for advancing the legitimist cause were seen as far-fetched, his impassioned moral voice commanded the utmost respect from the disparate Austrian émigré groups in Paris, which included, aside from the Monarchists, the Liberals, Socialists, Communists, backers of the controversial ex-Chancellor Schuschnigg, and still others. From 1935 to 1938, in his zeal to combat Hitler at all costs, he wrote for the organ of the Austrian semi-fascist Fatherland Front, *Der Christliche Ständestaat* (Vienna), and in his last year, 1939, for the monarchist newspaper *Die Österreichische Post* (Paris). He also wrote regularly for Leopold Schwarzschild's anti-Stalinist socialist journal, *Das Neue Tage-Buch* (Paris), and for the leftist-democratic *Pariser Tageszeitung,* both of which represented the emigration from Germany.[23]

As Roth championed the Habsburg cause ever more fervently, the Catholic sentiments he had manifested earlier grew increasingly more pronounced and at times found odd expression in his personal behavior—reportedly, he turned up at mass drunk—and in his writing. In 1934, the apocalyptic book-essay he had begun three years earlier, *Der Antichrist* (The Anti-Christ*),* marked the literary-journalistic culmination of his cultural and political conservatism. The one-time liberal social critic now vehemently attacked the Social-Democrats and Communists, whom he saw as materialistic, godless catalysts for the rise of Nazism. All the while, even as he drank suicidally and his health declined rapidly, he was unflagging in his practical, time-devouring efforts to aid the intellectual refugees fleeing from the Third Reich to Paris.

In the spring of 1939 Roth passed up two chances to gain entry to the United States and thereby escape the ever-growing Nazi threat. One came from an aid committee headed by Eleanor Roosevelt, the other from his American translator and the president of the American P.E.N. Club, Dorothy Thompson. By that time, however, as his letters attest, he was deep in personal despair and only awaiting his end. His last work, the novella *Die Legende vom heiligen Trinker* (1939; The Legend of the Holy Drinker), transforms the hopeless longings and bottomless sorrows of the writer and drinker Joseph Roth into the charmingly ambiguous story of the Paris *clochard* Andreas Kartak. After serving a prison term for a murder of passion, Kartak, once a coal miner in Polish Silesia, passes his days aimlessly under the bridges of the Seine. Through a chain of "miracles" he is set on the path of virtue, but he repeatedly gives in to worldly temptation. In the end, though, he dies blissfully in the chapel of Sainte Marie des Batignolles, believing that he has finally made good on his vow to an unnamed benefactor to leave two hundred francs as a tribute to Sainte Thérèse de Lisieux. In truth, however, in a bistro opposite the chapel, weakened by his wayward existence, he had mistaken a young, angelic girl of the same name for the saint. In his simplicity, he dies with the sigh: "Miss Thérèse!" To this, Roth's gently ironic narrator comments: "May God grant us all, all of us drinkers, such a good and easy death!"[24]

In stark contrast, Roth's own death was torturous. On 23 May 1939, after learning that his dramatist friend and fellow exile Ernst Toller had hanged himself in a New York hotel room, he collapsed in Café Tournon in Paris and was taken to Hôpital Necker. After four agonizing days he died there of pneumonia and delirium tremens. Later that year, *The Legend of the Holy Drinker* was published in Amsterdam, a sublime transfiguration of its author's woeful end.

# CHAPTER 2

# The Early Work, 1923–1924

## Beginnings of a Career

### The Spider's Web

Joseph Roth began his literary career in 1923 with the novel *Das Spinnennetz* (The Spider's Web). Little about this first work pointed to the master storyteller who would emerge at the turn of the decade, but in historical retrospect the book marks a distinctive beginning. A year earlier, Roth announced that he would end his newspaper job with the conservative *Berliner Börsen-Courier,* explaining that he wished to avoid having to deny what he defined at that time as his social-ist convictions—even though he never expressed these convictions through adherence to a political party or its ideology (*BR* 40). He then began writing for various liberal papers in Berlin, Vienna, and Prague, the most prominent among them being the *Prager Tagblatt.* In the fall of 1923 *The Spider's Web* began appearing serially in the Vienna socialist *Arbeiter-Zeitung.* Against the back-ground of the early 1920s in Berlin, where he had begun the novel, Roth depicted the social and political disruptions that gave rise to the Nazi movement and were to cause the downfall of the Weimar Republic.

Starting in the spring of 1920, Roth witnessed the turbulence of the times firsthand in Berlin. In January 1919 the Sparticist uprising had been put down by the army, and its ideological leaders, Rosa Luxemburg and Karl Liebknecht, were murdered in prison. The following months saw the establishment of a Soviet Republic in Bavaria and, four weeks later, its overthrow by federal armed forces. On 31 July 1919 the Weimar Constitution was adopted, but from the start its efficacy was dependent on the stability of coalition governments. Now, how-ever, the threat to the Republic came from the right. Disaffected Freikorps mem-bers, separated from the regular army as a result of the Versailles Treaty, staged an insurrection in Berlin in mid-March 1920 (the so-called Kapp Putsch) and set up a monarchist-agrarian government. Within a week, however, it collapsed under opposition from the army command, Berlin officialdom, and trade unions. Following the general elections of 6 June 1920, the Socialists were excluded from the new Weimar coalition, a move that cost the government its democratic majority. On 24 June 1922 the Jewish industrialist and cabinet minister Walther Rathenau, who had negotiated the Rapallo Treaty with Russia that April, was assassinated by nationalist conspirators. Still other political forces and events animate the plot of *The Spider's Web,* but it is within this general climate of conflict and upheaval that the novel plays itself out.

By 1967, when the novel was published for the first time as a book, the original newspaper version had long been forgotten and, in the critical commentaries and analyses of Roth's work, the literary-historical outlines of his early fiction were clearly set, or at least seemed so. Although broad stylistic and thematic features linked the "new" novel with the author's other early works, it became clear that *The Spider's Web* occupies a niche of its own. Above all, what distinguishes it is Roth's strikingly prescient treatment of the emerging Nazi movement and the viciousness of its leaders. Roth thus showed an unparalleled clearsightedness, even beyond that of such well-known authors as Ernst Toller, Heinrich Mann, and Alfred Döblin, whose political thinking was more sharply defined than his.

Among German writers, Roth remained to his last day one of the most impassioned and unswerving opponents of Hitler and the Third Reich. Already in the early 1920s, he had begun to write against the growing threat of the National Socialists; during his later exile years, when the threat had become reality, he raised his opposition to fever pitch. But he did this entirely as an essayist and journalist; nowhere in his fiction did he again portray the criminality of Nazism so concretely and directly as he did in *The Spider's Web,* nor did he create a central figure so thoroughly and irredeemably villainous as the novel's Theodor Lohse. Primarily for these reasons, *The Spider's Web* stands distinctly apart from the two books that quickly followed it in 1924, *Hotel Savoy* (Hotel Savoy) and *Die Rebellion* (Rebellion), as well as from the succeeding ones, *Die Flucht ohne Ende* (1927; Flight without End), *Zipper und sein Vater* (1928; Zipper and His Father), and *Rechts und Links* (1929; Right and Left).

Like the central figures in all five of these works, Roth's protagonist Lohse returns from the First World War to a civilian life in which he finds himself disoriented and malcontent. Unlike these other protagonists, however, who tend to be hesitant onlookers to life and events, but in the main genuine and likable, Lohse is driven by a brutal ambition, a lack of moral scruples, and a racial anti-Semitism that had become widespread among the middle class of the time. His destructive nature, as Roth traces it in the book's first chapter, develops early. Starting with his years as a timorous schoolboy from a petit-bourgeois family, Lohse is tormented by feelings of personal inadequacy, coupled with envy and resentment of those more gifted than he. Military duty relieves him of the need to think for himself, but once outside the ordered routine of army life he again feels painfully insecure. At first he studies law while earning his keep as tutor to the son of a wealthy Jew (to whose young wife he feels drawn despite his phobic anti-Semitism). Single-mindedly, he begins to forge his path to a role of power within the clandestine fascist right. Along the way, he subjects himself to misuse in the bed of a Prussian prince, murders a fellow conspirator, brutally suppresses a protest by exploited Polish farm workers—a 1921 revolt in Upper Silesia provided the motif—and, to further his social and political rise, marries the daughter of an aristocratic family (who is likewise motivated by personal ambition).

Ceaselessly grasping for political connections and manipulating others while being manipulated himself, Lohse first achieves local, then national, prominence. He manages to gain the attention of Ludendorff and even sees himself as a rival of Hitler, a shadowy figure who lurks in the background of the novel. Ironically, Lohse reaches the height of his climb to power, as chief of a still non-existent Reich security service, through the designs of an east European Jew from Lodz, the ruthlessly nihilistic Benjamin Lenz. Far keener of wit than Lohse, the double agent Lenz plays all sides against each other in his zeal to destroy western European society, whose institutions and values he despises. Abetting the aims of his "friend" for his own purposes, Lenz characterizes Lohse in terms that reflect not only his scorn for western civilization but also Roth's prevision of the Nazi monster. Lenz predicts of Lohse that he "would now beget sons who in their turn would become murderers, killers, Europeans, bloodthirsty and cowardly, warlike and nationalistic, bloody but churchgoing, believers in the European God who was worshipped through politics."[1]

Even as Lohse revels in his rising influence, he finds himself trapped in the spider's web of Nazi treachery and brutality, which he himself has helped weave. When he discovers Lenz copying secret party documents, he is humiliated by the recognition that he is powerless to expose him—Lenz knows that Lohse has spilled the blood of party rivals and effectively threatens him with disclosure. Thereupon, Lohse retreats submissively, and the novel concludes with the open end that would typify Roth's work thereafter. Benjamin Lenz prudently cautions his younger brother Lazar, a chemist working on explosives, to leave Germany and supplies him with money and a false passport. He himself remains behind on the empty train platform, while "[s]omewhere, many locomotives were whistling on the tracks" (*SW* 112).

Pithily, if somewhat glibly, the narrator says of Lohse in the book's first lines: "One might say that he exceeded expectations which he never had" (*SW* 3). In fact, Roth did succeed best in the novel at probing the personality of a quite ordinary burgher, who is driven inwardly and blindly to fulfill his visions of political power regardless of the moral cost. He also succeeded—though less effectively than his contemporaries Lion Feuchtwanger (1884–1958) or Alfred Döblin

(1878–1957), for example—in evoking the political and social turbulence that undermined the struggling Weimar Republic.[2] Party clashes and illegal agitation along the broad spectrum—from proto-Fascists on the right to Socialists and Communists on the left, furtive maneuvering within parties for position and favor, hostilities between the landed gentry and the rural proletariat, gaping inequities between the privileged and the socially dispossessed, inflation, and hunger—all interweave to create a dense atmospheric background to the novel.

Less successful is Roth's attempt to provide his story with epic sweep. Aiming for a vivid and varied panorama of time and place, he packs widely strewn developments, episodes, and events in sustained staccato rhythms within single long paragraphs—with the result that his quick-paced portrayal loses focus as well as depth. And, while Lohse as a central figure commands interest as the embodiment of a distinct individual psychology and political ideology, he is likewise portrayed too schematically to elicit a strong emotional response from the reader. Much the same can be said for Lohse's antagonist, Lenz. With his iron will bent on bringing down western Europe, his ruthlessness and matchless cunning, his uncanny ability to penetrate the highest circles and innermost chambers of power, and his fearless exploits across the political map, Lenz is plain implausible—as implausible as the image of the rootless, destructive, international Jew that was projected by the Nazi propaganda of the time. That Roth himself referred to his next novel, *Hotel Savoy,* as his first, could well attest to his own awareness that, for all of its inherent interest, *The Spider's Web* is structurally and stylistically flawed.

## Hotel Savoy

Until the book publication of *The Spider's Web* in 1967, *Hotel Savoy* (1924) had been regarded as Roth's first novel. Like its predecessor and other novels that were to follow, it had first run serially in a newspaper. In February and March of 1924 it appeared in the *Frankfurter Zeitung,* whose staff Roth had joined the year before. Later in 1924 it was published as a book, along with the author's third novel, *Rebellion,* which had first appeared as a serial in the Berlin newspaper *Vorwärts.*

*Hotel Savoy* is neither so explicitly political in its plot as *The Spider's Web,* nor is the more general theme of social protest so concentratedly developed as in *Rebellion.* What most immediately relates its central figure and first-person narrator, Gabriel Dan, to Theodor Lohse of *The Spider's Web* and other protagonists of Roth's early work, is Dan's personal situation, which remains constant throughout the novel. Like the others, he is a war veteran, looking solely toward his return to peacetime society. In this regard, he stands closest of all to Franz Tunda in *Flight without End*. Much like Tunda, Dan remains largely indifferent to the social currents that unsettle the postwar society he encounters on his journey westward. In *Hotel Savoy* these currents are represented most ominously by revolutionary agitation, which rumbles in the background of the novel until it finally erupts in fiery destruction.

Although Roth appears to have nourished larger thematic ambitions for the novel, he depicts Dan's story as a wholly private one; Lohse's rise and downfall, on the other hand, result from a fateful amalgam of his own perverted ambition with the fascist political movements in Weimar Germany, which themselves figure more prominently and convincingly in the plot structure than does the political subplot in *Hotel Savoy*. While Lohse, an early Nazi, sates his rage against the bourgeois values of the Weimar Republic, Dan is concerned merely with his return to the comforts of western Europe after three years of Russian war imprisonment. He intends his stay at Hotel Savoy, in an unnamed city "at the gates of Europe"—in reality, the city of Lodz in western Poland, where a Hotel Savoy still stands today—to be temporary, to last a few days or a week.[3] From local relatives of his Russian-Jewish parents he hopes for the money that will enable him to continue his journey home to Vienna.

By setting the largest part of the narrative either entirely or partially in Hotel Savoy itself, Roth intended to install the hotel as a major symbolic force in the novel. Describing the plight of the indigent guests who occupy the upper floors and are exploited ruthlessly by the elevator boy Ignatz, the narrator, Dan, reflects: "This Hotel Savoy was like the world. Brilliant light shone out from it and splendor glittered from its seven storeys, but poverty made its home in its high places, and those who lived on high were in the depths, buried in airy graves, and the graves were in layers above the comfortable rooms of the well nourished guests sitting down below, untroubled by the flimsy coffins overhead" (*HS* 33).

Clearly, Roth intended the hotel and its inner life to serve as a metaphor for the social corruption and decay of postwar Europe, but all in all he failed to realize his larger narrative aims. For this, his oddly surrealistic portrayal is much overworked. The furtive Ignatz (who in the end proves to be the feared, but never seen, Greek owner, Kaleguropulos), the motley assemblage of social outcasts who inhabit the upper floors of the hotel, the caricature-like figures from near and far who frequent the hotel bar, the hotel's interior trappings, descriptively contrived to reflect the hierarchy of material means among the guests—all were meant to mirror contemporary social conditions in western Europe. In their narrative composite, however, both the physical setting of the hotel and the figures who populate it are too fancifully drawn to project the symbolic picture Roth intended. With the fiery end of the hotel—which allows Roth to send Dan further on his way and thus conclude the novel—they cease to exist as bearers of meaning.

If one discounts the artificial aspects of Roth's depiction, the world of *Hotel Savoy* reveals itself as a historically familiar one. It encompasses, that is, a specific segment of secularized east European Jewry caught amid the social and economic disruptions that followed the First World War. Its members, but a step removed from their origins in the ghetto and Jewish shtetl, are would-be entrepreneurs of every stripe, middle-men with neither means nor clients, petty speculators, currency dealers, owners of run-down factories, and, further below them, artisans and artists of sorts. Civically emancipated, but estranged from their spiritual roots in traditional Judaism, they consume themselves with doggedly and fruitlessly pursuing the chance opportunities that promise to boost their shaky fortunes. Together, they constitute a new social and economic ghetto that finds its crystallization point in Hotel Savoy. Even its more successful members, like Dan's uncle Phöbus Böhlaug and his playboy son, Alexander, are marked by the emptiness of character and the abandonment to material values that Roth was to decry ever more insistently among what he saw as a westernized decadent Jewry.

The counterbalance to this loss of spiritual substance is provided by Henry Bloomfield, a former son of the town who has struck it rich in America and has now returned for his yearly visit. Anticipation of the fabulous Bloomfield's arrival excites hectic financial scheming and charity soliciting among his erstwhile townsmen. As Dan discovers, however, Bloomfield has not returned to transact business, but rather to visit the grave of his father, Jechiel Blumenfeld. To Dan he reveals what remains hidden from the cadgers and would-be entrepreneurs who press for his ear: "'I come here every year to visit my father,' says Bloomfield, 'and I cannot forget the town either. I am an Eastern Jew and, to us, home is above all where our dead lie. Had my father died in America I could be perfectly at home in America. My son will be a full-blooded American, because I shall be buried there'" (*HS* 107). The commentary that this confession evokes from Dan lends Bloomfield's words a deepened and singular significance: "Life and death hang together so visibly, and the quick with the dead. There is no end there, no break—always continuity and connection" (*HS* 107).

This insight comes unexpectedly from Dan. It expresses a conviction that is entirely lacking in all of his actions, and the very cadence of pronouncement is foreign to his speech. Such a palpable shift in narrative stance suggests that Roth was voicing a personal conviction through Dan. Given that Roth had grown up in the home of his orthodox maternal grandfather, Jechiel Grübel—with whom Bloomfield's father, significantly, shares the first name—it is more than likely

21

that this ethos of generational continuity had been instilled in him through family observance and custom. It is just as likely that it had been reinforced by the Jewish community tradition in which his native Brody was steeped. Either knowingly or unawares, through his character Gabriel Dan he formulated the central principle of Jewish existence that the religious philosopher Martin Buber described metaphorically as the "chain of generations." Speaking in the fateful year of 1933 in the Stuttgart *Jüdisches Lehrhaus,* Buber revealed the vast historical perspective of this thought. Recalling his visits to the ancient Jewish cemetery in Worms, he said:

> Down below there is not an iota of form. One had only the stones and the ashes beneath the stones. One has the ashes, however much they have dissolved. One has the corporality of the people who have turned into them. One has it. I have it. I do not have it as a corporality within the confines of this planet but as the embodiment of my own memory reaching into the depths of history, right back to Sinai.
>
> I stood there, united with the ashes and through them with my forefathers. This is the memory of the encounter with God, which is given to all Jews . . .
>
> I stood there and experienced everything myself. I suffered all the deaths: All the ashes, all the destruction, all the silent lamentation are mine; but the covenant was not withdrawn from me.[4]

Where the individual Jew stands in the present, Roth affirms in the novel, countless others stood earlier; through personal remembrance he secures and hallows the bond with his forebears. When Dan later avers that he had understood Bloomfield, that they shared the same emotion of homesickness, he recognizes only part of the deeper metaphysical truth that he himself had expressed.

By introducing into the plot Dan's former comrade-in-arms, the social insurgent Zwonimir Pansin, who leads an uprising of workers and war returnees against their exploiters, Roth sought to portray the social forces that threatened the capitalist decadence embodied in the hotel. But, despite Dan's sympathy with the rebels' cause, he remains an onlooker, eager to continue his journey to Vienna, and the sketchily drawn revolutionary events leave little imprint on the reader.

Given the ineffectiveness of this subplot, one may contend that *Hotel Savoy* could have become a more engrossing and persuasive novel had Roth intently pursued the Jewish theme that so clearly occupied him. For whatever reason, however, he let this opportunity slip by. Indeed, except for his noteworthy character portrayal of the Russian-born "half-Jew" Nikolai Brandeis in *Right and Left* (1929), Roth all but abandoned the Jewish theme in the five novels that followed *Hotel Savoy.* When he returned to it six years later in *Job,* it permeated the entire work.

## Rebellion

Like Gabriel Dan, Andreas Pum, the protagonist of Roth's third novel, *Rebellion* (1924), is an Austrian war returnee. His story, however, takes place in Vienna (the intended goal of Dan's westward journey) and introduces a new theme into Roth's fiction: the futile protest of the individual against the social injustices that batter his existence. The terse language and critical, often ironic tone that typify Roth's third-person narration make themselves felt from the very start. The patients at Military Hospital Nr. 24—some blind, some lame, others awaiting an amputation—are too damaged by battle to reach the last stop of the trolley that could take them from the outskirts of the city back into its center and therewith to life. The mood among them is sullen and bleak. The invalid Pum, however, takes naive satisfaction in knowing that for the loss of his leg the government has rewarded him with a medal. Little does he suspect that in civilian life he will not only have to struggle against his physical disability but also assert himself against the prejudices of society's whole and healthy members. Since he believes unswervingly in God's justice as well as that of the government, he awaits the support of both in his efforts to gain personal security and dignity. Soon, however, mounting misfortune will disabuse him of his belief in justice and order and place it in ironic contrast to the central tenet of the novel, which throughout posits the exploitation of the weak and disinherited of society by its privileged or merely ruthless and cunning members. Pum's inevitable disillusionment will eventually grow too powerful for him to overcome.

As long as Pum can uphold his unquestioning faith in both divine and civil justice, he remains shielded against insight into the inequities of the society to which he has returned. Thus, he is unable to comprehend the rebellious spirit of his fellow patients at the veterans hospital. For him, they are "heathens," enemies of the government, without "God, Emperor, or Fatherland."[5] Naive as his notion of heathenry may be—indeed, because it represents a rationalization of his plight—Pum must cling to it: "It absolved him of the necessity of continuing to reflect any further and to think about the others. At the same time, it gave him a feeling of superiority to his comrades" (*R* 3). And, since for Pum the term heathen also describes persons "who are in prison, or perhaps still at large" (*R* 3), when he himself is jailed, albeit unjustly, he is fated to become a heathen in his own eyes.

Among the hospital patients, Pum is the only one to enjoy the harmony between what he falsely perceives to be a benevolent providence and the world of the "poor buggers," as a fellow patient more realistically views their generation of war veterans (*R* 5). Despite his battle injury and the deprivations he suffers on his return to civilian life, he finds the world agreeably intact; his government's justice is the earthly counterpart of divine justice. Even when he is discharged from the hospital with an organ grinder's license rather than the postage stamp concession or the position as a park or museum guard for which he had hoped, Pum's faith in a higher order reconciles him to his situation. The license, after all, like his medal, had been issued by the government "in person," and despite his unfulfilled hopes Pum can feel that he has been placed on equal footing with the authorities, whom he categorically respects (*R* 22). These are the illusions necessary to maintain his sense of personal freedom and security in the face of a hostile society, which the narrator empathetically and, at the same time, ominously, describes as "the enemy of us all" (*R* 21). While Pum rejoices in his strokes of seeming good luck—his livelihood as an organ grinder and his marriage to the newly widowed Katharina Blumich—Roth sets in motion a series of chance occurrences that fatefully combine, directly and indirectly, to plunge his protagonist undeservedly into misfortune.

Thanks to an altercation in the trolley car with the well-heeled, but on this particular day ill-tempered, businessman Herr Arnold, Pum loses his work license "in the name of the law" (*R* 64) and is sentenced to prison.[6] The injustice of his punishment persuades him that he has been abandoned by God, and for the first time he gains insight into the nature of his fate. Against his own will, he now sees himself as a heathen and realizes that his belief in God, justice, and the government had been illusory. In mute dialogue with the birds that fly to his cell window, he expresses this new recognition in words that have failed him until this turn of events: "[M]y feeble intellect was betrayed by my parents, my school, my teachers, by the Sergeant Major and the Captain, and the newspapers I was given to read. . . . I obeyed the laws of my country because I supposed wiser heads than mine had thought of them, and a great justice administered them in the name of our Lord and Creator" (*R* 116).

Pum now knows with certainty that the government has "all the earthly weaknesses and no line to God" (*R* 108). His generation had gone off to war for a higher cause, as he had believed, and returned to an unholy present. When, in the name of order, the unfeeling, bureaucratic prison administration refuses Pum's properly submitted request for a ladder that will allow him to feed the birds at his window, Pum equates order with imprisonment. Everywhere in life, he feels, a thousand prisons now await him. His angry recognition of the omnipresence of injustice shapes his return to society as a rebel "against the world, against the authorities, against the Government, against God" (*R* 119).

Pum's rebellion, however, is not driven by the will of a forceful battler for justice and order but rather by the bitter defiance of a man grown prematurely old and incapable of starting a new life. Released from prison, betrayed and abandoned by his crude, calculating wife, he again finds himself alone in the world. In a mirror he sees that during the short weeks of his internment his brown hair and beard have grown white. The mirror image prefigures Pum's approaching death, the knowledge of which now becomes his constant companion. As a toilet attendant in the Vienna Café Hallili, he sits "surrounded by blue tiled walls and full-length mirrors" (R 129), constantly faced, that is, with the reflection of his decline.

Helpless to rebel against the laws of society, on receiving still another court summons, Pum rebels against God, the highest and at the same time sole power that is still accessible to him. Fervently, Pum declares God guilty of the sufferings of humankind that occur in God's name. And, because untold millions innocently fall victim to God's injustice, the one individual, Andreas Pum, defiantly refuses God's mercy. Pum exclaims: "I want to go to hell" (R 142).

Although the dying invalid's rebellious rejection of God's order takes place in the most mundane of settings, the men's toilet of Café Hallili, and is pronounced in the delirium of a fatal illness, it achieves the passion and eloquence of the biblical Job story (which clearly stands as the model for it); moreover, the very act of rebellion bestows grace on Andreas Pum. For it releases him in *dignity* not only from the demeaning confinement of his work as a toilet attendant but also from the cruelties of his existence altogether.

This protest provides a point of departure for those Roth commentators who emphasize the novel's social criticism as its main theme. While the profane, pessimistic tone of the novel does not invalidate Pum's rebellion, it does drive home the fact that the protest of one "poor bugger," however moving, cannot alleviate the social injustice Roth wished to condemn through his protagonist's story. This is confirmed at the end of the novel, when the small-time criminal Willi, Pum's old roommate, pays his last respects to Pum, whose unclaimed remains are lying in the Anatomical Institute of Vienna University (where they will serve the ends of medical science). About to shed a tear, Willi—who has meanwhile assumed the "organization of all cloakrooms, ladies' and gentlemen's toilets'" (R 124)— begins whistling instead and goes off "to find an old man for the toilet" (R 143). Roth's bitterly ironic conclusion underscores that in a society bare of humane values the injustice against which Andreas Pum rebelled will continue and still others will fall victim to it.

# CHAPTER 3

# The Early Work, 1927–1929

## New Objectivism and Its Limits

### Flight without End

Despite his auspicious start as a novelist, until the mid-1920s Roth earned his livelihood chiefly as a journalist. He pursued his newspaper career vigorously, publishing hundreds of articles and feuilletons in socialist and liberal newspapers in Vienna, Prague, and Berlin. Soon, however, he was writing almost exclusively for the *Frankfurter Zeitung,* and as a prized contributor he regularly received choice assignments. In the fall of 1925, for example, readers saw the first of his signature travel reports, the ten-part series "Im mittäglichen Frankreich" (In the South of France). That same year he authored a second series from southern France, "Die weißen Städte" (The White Cities). It, too, consisted of ten articles, but they were considerably longer than those of the first series and were intended to be a book with fictional elements. However, they did not see publication until 1956, when an incomplete version was mistakenly included in Roth's *Werke* as part of "Im mittäglichen Frankreich."[1]

In both series, Roth reveled in a culture whose present still testified eloquently to both its pre-Christian and medieval-Catholic past. Throughout his journeys, which took him to a dozen cities, he responded acutely to the manifold, subtly nuanced stimuli of an organically evolved civilization. Above all, in Avignon he discovered to his profound delight an incomparably humane European Catholic culture which had assimilated into the present diverse ancient races while nourishing the individuality of each. Even in the port city of Marseilles, where his senses are beset by the hectic day-and-night whirl of traffic in goods and, along the harbor, women's bodies, he felt the historical energy of centuries compressed into the fleeting moment. In a letter to Benno Reifenberg, the feuilleton editor of the *Frankfurter Zeitung,* Roth explained significantly that the book he planned to write as a result of his journey would be "objective to the highest degree" because it would be "entirely 'subjective' . . . the 'confession' of a young man, skeptical and resigned . . . who sees the last remnants of a Europe that still have no inkling of Europe's steadily increased Americanization and Bolshevization" (*BR* 62).

Further assignments for the *Frankfurter Zeitung* between 1926 and 1928 resulted in several more travel sequences from countries in both western and eastern Europe, including Germany, the Soviet Union, Albania, Poland, and Italy. In 1927 Roth also published a book-essay, *Juden auf Wanderschaft* (*The Wandering Jews*), on a subject close to his heart: the east European Jews, whose everyday existence, in all of its varied aspects, he knew intimately from his earliest years to the time of his young manhood.[2] In the essay Roth vividly evokes the life of the *Ostjuden* in both their traditional small towns in the east of Europe and in the western urban ghettos to which their migrations took them: Vienna, Berlin, and Paris; throughout he passionately defends them and their cultural values against the manifold prejudices in the west that warped their image. In light of this predominantly journalistic output, the author's early accomplishments as a novelist are all the more remarkable.

Hard on the heels of *The Spider's Web, Hotel Savoy,* and *Rebellion,* there followed another three novels: *Flight without End* (1927), *Zipper and His Father* (1928), and *Right and Left* (1929). Taken together, these six books can be seen as the coherent early stage of Roth's fictional work. In part, this coherence is created by the motif that is central to all six: Like Roth himself, their protagonists are veterans of the First World War; at the outset of their respective stories, they are—with two exceptions—either on the way back from war service to their homes in Austria or Germany or they have newly returned there. In the generational novels *Right and Left* and *Zipper and His Father,* Roth varied this scheme by first depicting the prewar lives of his central figures against the background of their family histories before pursuing their stories in the present. In broad terms, the plot in every one of these novels but *Hotel Savoy* revolves around the protagonist's misfortunes as he unsuccessfully attempts to gain a foothold in the radically altered society to which he has returned.

The autobiographical, or pseudo-autobiographical, features in these early novels are apparent. In addition to army service, Roth wove into the lives of his protagonists still other elements of his own life story, including some of his fanciful variations of it. To Franz Tunda of *Flight without End,* for example, Roth assigned the rank of first lieutenant in the Austrian army and made of him a Russian war prisoner who subsequently fought in the Bolshevik Revolution— deeds Roth later falsely claimed of himself. Furthermore, he describes Tunda's father much like one of the sundry father figures he invented for himself, as a non-Jew and major in the Austrian army. Closer to the truth of his own life, he endows Tunda with a Polish-Jewish mother, although this circumstance bears no import whatsoever for Tunda's fortunes, nor does it affect his self-awareness. Along with Gabriel Dan of *Hotel Savoy,* whose personal experience is deepened by his Jewish identity, and, later, Paul Bernheim of *Right and Left,* for whom the fact of his Jewish birth proves negligible, Tunda is still another of the many Jewish or partly Jewish persons who inhabit Roth's books as either central figures or key secondary characters. Despite Roth's early efforts to distance himself from his Galician origins, his work shows clearly that his family circumstances and upbringing continued to affect him well beyond the years of his difficult youth in Brody. In ever-varying mutations, both the anxious, overly solicitous mother, whom he lost early in life, and the father he had never known entered his fiction.

Beyond the similarities of their core motifs, however, it was Roth's critical depiction of postwar European bourgeois society that links these six novels thematically and—with the notable exception of the villainous Theodor Lohse in *The Spider's Web*—makes their protagonists brothers under the skin. Gabriel Dan, to be sure, remains in transition between his recent military past and the civilian life that awaits him, but the others must all contend with their impotence in an inimical world not of their own making. After the war experiences that altered the moral consciousness of their entire generation, they live as onlookers in an oppressive condition of temporariness or, in pursuing their inflated ambitions, they accept equally oppressive forms of personal compromise. In their own eyes, as in those of Roth, they represent a lost generation, and in this regard Roth's early novels strike a decidedly original note amid the German fiction of the Weimar period. To be certain, they show thematic ties with, say, Alfred Döblin's *Berlin Alexanderplatz* (1929), Erich Kaestner's *Fabian* (1931), and Hans Fallada's *Kleiner Mann- was nun* (1932); but these are, above all, novels of social uprootedness whereas Roth specifically situated his main figures as war returnees, whose postwar disillusionment and sense of futility relate them more to their American counterparts in the novels of Ernest Hemingway and F. Scott Fitzgerald than to their German ones.[3]

Beginning with *Flight without End,* Roth expanded the plot and setting of his novels to open a broad view onto central and western European society in the post–World War I period. In *Flight without End* he also employed for the first time the documentary style that led contemporary and later critics to view him— along with such writers as E. Kästner, H. Kesten, E. Glaeser, and K. Tucholsky— as a foremost representative of the activist literary movement *Neue Sachlichkeit* (New Objectivism).[4] This rather amorphous movement, which had arisen in Berlin in the early 1920s in opposition to the extreme subjectivity and emotiveness of late expressionism, championed a new realism of firsthand, analytic observation. Its proponents endorsed the documentary and biographical or autobiographical novel and eyewitness accounts of social conditions as the sole adequate means for portraying the great evils of the contemporary western world. These evils included the First World War, renascent militarism, fascism, modern technology, and social corruption and decay. Roth's preface to *Flight without*

*End* was commonly cited as a proclamation of the literary principles of New Objectivism. Writing above his own name, he declared:

> In what follows, I tell the story of my friend and comrade and spiritual associate, Franz Tunda.
>
> I follow in part his notes, in part his narrative.
>
> I have invented nothing, made up nothing. The question of "poetic invention" is no longer relevant. Observed fact is all that counts.
>
> Paris, March 1927                                          Joseph Roth[5]

Ironically enough, two years later in a feuilleton for the *Frankfurter Zeitung* titled "Es lebe der Dichter" (Long Live the Poet), Roth declared that the critics had absolutely misunderstood him, that his preface to the novel had nothing to do with "the 'celebrated' New Objectivism, which tended to equate documentary writing with artlessness" (*W* 4:224). Nonetheless, to further establish his fiction as non-fiction—to authenticate his "Report," as Roth subtitled the novel—he employed a number of stylistic devices that allowed him to figure directly in the story as its eyewitness author-narrator. Most of chapter 9, for example, is taken up with an account of one of Tunda's earlier experiences in the Caspian port city of Baku, which the author-narrator has personally extracted from Tunda's diary. Intermittently, the author-narrator turns up himself, reporting in the first person as Tunda's "friend"; in Berlin the author-narrator personally accompanies Tunda through the city's streets, bars, and cafés, and acquaints him with the city's avant-garde artist circles. At one point Tunda writes a chapter-long letter, describing his life in the Caucusus, to the author-narrator (chap. 11), and, later in the novel, Tunda authors an unfinished, pseudonymously published book on his Siberian experiences, to which the author-narrator supplies a foreword (chap. 23).

Roth begins *Flight without End* with Franz Tunda's escape from Russian war imprisonment in Siberia and briefly relates his uneventful three-year abode in Siberia with the reclusive Polish hunter Baranowicz. He then narrates Tunda's trek westward in the spring of 1919, his sojourn in Russia and, under the influence of his Russian lover, Natasha Alexandrovna, his involvement in the Revolution as a Red Army member. When Tunda recognizes the bourgeois banality that underlies Alexandrovna's revolutionary zeal—in which Roth also mirrors the post-Revolutionary society that so thoroughly disillusioned him during his Russian travels in 1926[6]—he breaks with Alexandrovna and retreats to the Caucusus. Here and in Baku he lives a secluded life with his young half-Georgian wife, Alja, but once her simple ways lose their charm, he deserts her and finally returns to his native Austria.

Vienna, too, however, proves to be only another way station on the "flight without end" that characterizes Tunda's postwar existence and gives the book its title. Having learned that his former fiancée Irene Hartmann had ceased waiting for him and married four years earlier, he leaves Vienna and travels to Germany. There he stays with his brother, George, an orchestra conductor in a small Rhenish city, where he is repulsed by the conformism, vacuity, and pretense of the middle-class and artist circles to which he is introduced. After a brief interlude in Berlin, which he experiences as an artificial enclave rife with incongruity and decadence, he moves on to Paris. Here, he is lured by the hope of meeting up with Hartmann and by romantic ambitions kindled by Madame G., a French woman he had met in Baku. However, among the upper crust of Parisian society he encounters the same spiritual emptiness and moral bankruptcy as in Germany.

In Paris, the plot of the novel reaches the open end that had already come to typify Roth's fictional writing. Still longing for an undefined inner fulfillment, Tunda is pictured standing alone and resigned at the Place de la Madeleine, "in the center of the capital city of the world," at a loss for what to do with his life. The narrator comments bleakly, "He had no occupation, no desire, no hope, no ambition, and not even any self-love. No one in the whole world was as superfluous as he" (*FE* 144). With these final words, Roth extends Tunda's "flight without end" beyond the conclusion of his story into an uncertain, unpromising future.

## Zipper and His Father

Appearing in 1928, *Zipper and His Father* continued in the documentary mode of *Flight without End*. Here, too, Roth introduces his own person into the novel as an authenticating eyewitness narrator. The last chapter, in fact, can be read as a demonstration of the aesthetic tenets of New Objectivism. It contains a conversation between Roth and Eduard P., a figure bordering on the mysterious, who regularly turns up at the same artists and writers' coffee house frequented by Roth and his boyhood friend Arnold Zipper. The conversation centers on Zipper's failure in life, but also develops into a discussion on the art of the novel and in particular the narrative possibilities of a novel on Arnold Zipper. In response to Roth's ironic claim that if he wished to write a novel about Arnold Zipper he would be unable to depict him in isolation from his father, P. comments:

> Now there you're right! . . . The Zippers belong together. Look at the father. He is responsible for Arnold's misfortune, [in the event that Arnold is still unhappy, SR]. But that's beside the point. All of our fathers are responsible for our bad luck. Our fathers belong to the generation which made the war. . . .

Just think back: You came back, the unluckiest generation of the modern era. . . . You'd hardly come home before your fathers were sitting again in the chairs they had at the outbreak of the war. They made the newspapers, public opinion, the peace treaties, politics. You young people were a thousand times more competent, but exhausted, half dead and needing to rest. You had no means of earning a living. It made no difference whether you had lived or died. And to *what* did you come home? To your parents' houses![7]

P.'s indictment of the fathers' generation articulates in summary the theme that Roth had already developed in his novel: the inability of the sons to find their way back from the war trenches to civilian life, and the guilt of the fathers for their tragic failure. To substantiate this view of the fateful relationship between the two generations, Roth devoted his first seven chapters to a portrait of the Zipper family. At the family's center stands the elder Zipper, in whom Roth created one of the most colorful of the many memorable figures that enliven his work. As a boy, the narrator tells us, from time to time he had looked to Zipper as a substitute for the father that he himself had never known. Years later, memories of this "sad clown," as Roth calls him, still enchanted the writer's imagination. Roth depicts him so affectionately in all of his gentle petit-bourgeois eccentricities and comical ineptitude that the reader could well overlook Zipper's decidedly darker qualities, above all the despotic pettiness to which he subjects his long-suffering wife and the destructive disdain he levels at his wayward son, Caesar.

Charging himself with having failed in life, the elder Zipper laments to narrator Roth that he "had been forced to spend the greater part of the energy that God had bestowed on him in making a bourgeois out of his proletarian self" (*ZF* 131). To compensate for the successes he never achieved, he cherishes extravagant ambitions for his son Arnold. Because Caesar, Arnold's dull-witted younger brother, proves unfit for success of any kind—he later dies insane—Arnold was to fulfill the dreams that the elder Zipper himself had failed to realize. These dreams are reflected in the photographs of Arnold that crowd the walls of the Zipper "salon." Here the visitor can admire Arnold from babyhood on in a dazzling array of costumes, as dragoon and sailor, as cyclist and equestrian, as pianist and violinist, as archer and fencer. Steeped in constant twilight, smelling of moth balls, crammed with the bricabrac of sunken yesterdays, and reserved for Sunday use only, the Zipper salon reflects a life invested in the quest for bourgeois respectability, but crowned only with the most modest and ephemeral of successes (*ZF* 118–120). In describing the abundantly revealing salon, it is as though Roth anticipated quite early P.'s damning reference to the parental houses to which their lost generation had returned, and applied it as a symbol of the tragedy of this generation. Whether Roth conceived of this strategy prior to writing or it developed as he wrote the novel, he followed it literally. In essence, the conversation with P. is one of the author, Roth, with himself, an ironic discourse on the fate of Arnold Zipper as well as the aesthetics of New Objectivism.

After Roth and his friend Arnold return from war service, a Vienna coffee house frequented by artists and writers replaces the Zipper home as the narrative setting for their chance encounters. The younger Zipper retreats regularly to the coffee house in order to escape his unnerving loneliness. But he also seeks refuge there from any reminder of the bourgeois world in which he was reared and, thanks to his father's intervention, now pursues his livelihood as a thoroughly alienated minor official in the Office of Taxation. What the Viennese critic and feuilletonist Alfred Polgar (1873–1955) once wrote of the famed literary meeting place Café Central describes perfectly the escapist function of the coffee house for Arnold Zipper: "Vienna's 'Café Central,'" Polgar observed, "is no coffee house like other coffee houses, but rather a *Weltanschauung* [lit. a way of viewing the world, SR], and in particular one whose innermost content consists in avoiding any look at the world. What can one see there anyway?"[8] But even as Arnold seeks to escape his father's world, he replicates the negative social patterns that typify it. The artists and writers' coffee house in which he frets away his evening hours merely offers a more sophisticated setting for futility than the plain neighborhood one where his father kills three hours daily amidst the company of card and billiard players.

For both Zippers the coffee house provides a haven from the oppressiveness of their empty existences. The son, however, is fleeing a world not of his own, but of his father's doing, and thus he finds it all the more unbearable. Whereas the elder Zipper persists in the belief that, thanks to his useless preoccupations and chance connections, he has stood the test of life successfully, Arnold proves thoroughly unequal to the life for which the older generation predestined him. He malingers at his job in the Finance Ministry, and soon quits it. Out of despair he falls in love with the aspiring stage actress Erna Wilder, a childhood sweetheart whom he had lost sight of ten years earlier. From this time on, he slavishly devotes himself to serving Wilder's career. Once married, he follows her from one provincial theater to the next and finally to Berlin. As she unscrupulously pursues a film career, he restlessly chases down opportunities to sing her praises as the film editor of a small paper. He endures her indifference, her costly tastes, and, in the end, even her marital betrayals with lovers of both sexes.

To create the semblance of a halfway secure bourgeois existence, as his father had done, exceeds Arnold's capacities. When Wilder returns to film acting after a severe illness that sent her fortunes into decline, he finds himself abandoned. At first he stays above water by playing the violin in a café in Nice, where he had followed Wilder—only to be deserted by her once more. Finally, after a stint as musical straight man for the stage clown Lock—modeled after the renowned, real-life Brock—he ends up on the vaudeville stage. There he consciously plays the clown that his now deceased father had always been without knowing it.

In the "Letter of the Author to Arnold Zipper," with which the novel concludes, Roth himself explains the significance of his friend's new profession. "It is symbolic," he writes, "of our generation of returned soldiers, whom everyone hinders in our attempts to play a part, make a decision, play a violin. We will never be able to make ourselves understood, my dear Arnold, in the way that your father still could. We have been decimated. There are not enough of us" (*ZF* 244–45). Although the letter follows the last page of the novel, like Roth's conversation with P., it belongs to the narrative structure. It, too, is intended to underscore the exemplary nature of the story and, in the spirit of New Objectivism, to authenticate it as biography. Beyond this, however, Roth sees in Arnold Zipper's lot, as he himself explains, a reflection of his own isolation and impotence as a writer. For he must fear that his readers will misapprehend his novel as a "mere reporting of two private lives," whereas he had attempted to portray in it the larger question of the fateful similarities and differences between two generations (*ZF* 244).

Roth regards the symbolism of Zipper's new profession as a less refined, but clearer variant of the symbolism he sees in his own vocation as a writer. Much as Zipper must clown at violin playing before an audience unreceptive to the sorrows of his existence, Roth feels himself frustrated by a readership unable to appreciate his artistic aims. In laying claim to the authenticity of a report at the expense of the truths unique to narrative invention, Roth confesses his inability to portray the fate of the war generation in a novel that flows from belief in the validity of storytelling.

## Right and Left

When Roth's next novel, *Right and Left,* appeared in 1929, he had already abandoned the narrative principles of New Objectivism. To be sure, in this work, too, he thematizes his criticism of postwar European society, but the earlier intimacy of the author-narrator with his protagonist, which underscored the "reality" of the two previous novels, no longer plays a part in its structure.

Paul Bernheim, the central figure of *Right and Left,* is portrayed as already being an ambitious and pretentious weakling in his youth. His interests flutter between art and literature, dancing and fencing, romantic infatuation and regular visits to a brothel. He goes off to war as though to a costume ball, and although his experiences at the front teach him for the first time to value life, he returns home essentially unchanged. The shallow values of his bourgeois upbringing and education have molded his character beyond reform and placed a meaningful existence beyond his reach. His path to a supposedly secure position in higher society is paved with hypocrisy, deception, and subservience. Contrary to his visions of success, the young banker Bernheim ends in total self-surrender to the bidding of others. His marriage to Irmgard Enders, the daughter of an industrial family, ties him to a wife he is unable to love and turns him into a puppet of her powerful uncle, Carl Enders, who bends Bernheim to his own will. Ultimately, however, Roth's criticism is not leveled against Bernheim, who is held captive in his marriage, but rather against the ruthless, exploitative industrialist Carl Enders, and, even more tellingly, against the spiritual and intellectual hollowness of the social caste that Enders represents and to which Bernheim aspires.

More than the unanticipated success of *Right and Left*, it was evidently Roth's own discomfort with the rambling novel that prompted him to claim that his readers had misconstrued the work. In an article of 22 November 1929 for the Berlin journal *Literarische Welt*, ironically titled "Selbstverriß" (Panning Myself), Roth argues that "right and left" had not been intended to describe genuine political positions, that at most his book only touched on questions of what he disdainfully termed "primitive politics."[9] Denying any attempt at psychological portrayal, he charges the contemporary reader with falsely understanding literature as a reproduction of life rather than as a purely artistic product of language. However, his rather forced arguments fail to resolve the discrepancy between the novel's programmatic title and its conspicuously disjointed plot. In fact, after Bernheim passes through a wartime phase as a pacifist and halfhearted revolutionary, he pursues his goals on the political right—as does his personally less gifted brother, Theodor. And neither of the two finds an adversary on the left whose role might help to concretize the novel's title.

Like his namesake, Theodor Lohse in *The Spider's Web*, the younger Bernheim brother entangles himself in the plottings of the fascist right. However, under the scornful patronage of the Russian-Jewish financial adventurer Nikolai Brandeis, the anti-Semitic Theodor eventually enters the employ of a Jewish-owned liberal newspaper and thus betrays the allegiances he had sworn to the ideology of "blood and iron."[10] All in all, then, Roth falls short of his aim to represent in him the revanchist "generation of the younger brothers" that spawned the assassin of the German foreign minister Walther Rathenau in 1922 and hastened the end of the Weimar Republic (*BR* 116). Moreover, the stories of both

Bernheims become overshadowed by that of the inscrutable, fabulously successful Brandeis, who dominates the second part of the novel almost completely before he quits the scene of action as unexpectedly as he had entered it. Despite Roth's protestations of authorial purpose in his *"Selbstverriß,"* it seems as though in the process of writing he had become unsure of his subject and that the design of the novel had slipped from his grasp.

It testifies to the artistic crisis in which Roth found himself during these years that in January 1930 he published a lengthy, often cited article titled "Schluß mit der 'Neuen Sachlichkeit'!" (Enough of "Neue Sachlichkeit"!).[11] In it he echoes the argument he had advanced two years earlier in "Long Live the Poet"; he decries the confusion common among German critics and readers between report and event; that is, he rejects the then widely accepted claim of the writer-reporter to objectivity, and with it the tenet of New Objectivism that genuine literature must be documentary. The facts, Roth argues, are the crude material of writing; as such they must be legitimized through language. The observations of the writer as eyewitness must be filtered through an artistic temperament. Taking as his example a train crash that the reader has personally witnessed and playing on the theoretical concepts of New Objectivism, Roth argues:

> Only an artistic [*künstlerisch*] report of a train crash (any train crash) will appear to the reader as a "true" account of the misfortune that he himself experienced. The "artistic report" attains the level on which details are unnecessary to render it valid. The eyewitness's account was "authentic." But in the reader it failed to attain even the level of credibility because the eyewitness was a (chance) participant in the event and thus can *only* recognize the true immediacy of his impressions in the "poetic" immediacy of the artistically shaped report, and not in the unshaped simplicity of the "documentary" report. What appears to attest to "life" itself is far removed both from the "inner" or "higher truth," but also from the power of reality. Only the "work of art" is as "genuine as life itself."[12]

Despite Roth's own earlier, at least seeming pledges of allegiance to New Objectivism, his novels of this period often evidence the creative subjectivity that the adherents of the movement proscribed but that he championed in "Schluß mit der 'Neuen Sachlichkeit'!"

## *The Silent Prophet* and *Perlefter*

In 1966 a previously unknown novel by Roth appeared under the title *Der stumme Prophet* (The Silent Prophet).[13] Owing to certain biographical congruities between the central figure, Friedrich Kargan, and the Russian social revolutionary Leon Trotsky, the book has been frequently referred to as Roth's "Trotsky novel." It derived its title, however, from that of an excerpt Roth had published as a story in 1929 in the Berlin literary journal *Neue Rundschau.* (Earlier that year, another excerpt had appeared under the title "Ein Kapitel Revolution" [A Chapter from the Revolution] in an anthology edited by Herman Kesten.)[14] The later book version was pieced together, in a painstaking editorial process, from three separate manuscripts that had been discovered in the Roth Archive of the Leo Baeck Institute in New York.

Most probably, Roth worked on the projected novel in the years 1927–1929, but then abandoned the undertaking. Its narrative technique of "anti-fiction," which includes long excerpts from the protagonist's diary, aligns it closely with the other novels of social protest, commencing with *Flight without End,* that Roth published during these same years. In *The Silent Prophet* too, however, his faithfulness to the tenets of New Objectivism was at best a matter of degree. Despite passages that convincingly display Roth's gifts of wit and language (and a nicely wrought, wistful love story), the novel—parts of which remain decidedly in the rough—succeeds less well than did its predecessors. Stylistically, it is altogether uneven, and its protagonist, Friedrich Kargan, lacks the flesh-and-blood presence that might make of him as memorable a figure as, say, the elder Zipper in *Zipper and His Father.*

Born in Odessa as the illegitimate son of an Austrian piano teacher and the daughter of a Russian tea merchant, Kargan is soon sent with his mother to a well-to-do uncle in Triest, where he spends his childhood. Denied a gymnasium education, he works for a shipping company and, thanks to his diligence and language abilities, is transferred to a branch office along the Austrian-Russian border—a region that was to become the site of several of Roth's future novels. Later, in Vienna, where he completes the gymnasium and studies at the university, the young Kargan sympathizes with the goals of communism and takes part in subversive actions, both there and in the border region he had come to know earlier. After long, often perilous and doubt-ridden service in the cause of the Russian Revolution, he decides to join his banished comrades in Siberian exile rather than acquiesce to the betrayal of the ideals of the Revolution by the party functionaries. Behind Kargan's ideological adversary, the swarthy Caucasian party leader Savelli, there visibly lurks the image of Stalin, and Roth's anticipation of the Stalinist purges attests strikingly to his insights into the perversions of dictatorship. In the end, however, it must be questioned whether Roth himself would have wished to see his shelved attempts at a novel printed in their present book form.

Just as questionable was the publication in 1978 of *Perlefter: Die Geschichte eines Bürgers* (Perlefter: The Story of a Bourgeois).[15] Described on its title page as the "fragment of a novel from [Roth's] Berlin literary remains," the work consists of ten chapters that turned up in two cardboard boxes in Berlin, in what was then still East Germany, and were then assembled somewhat like a jigsaw puzzle. In actuality, the first chapter was intended by Roth for another, likewise unfinished work, and has scant connection to the story of the title figure of the "novel," Alexander Perlefter.[16] But Perlefter himself barely has a story. Rather, the lusterless book consists almost entirely of a series of character portraits from the Jewish middle class of a city that appears to be Vienna, and all too often these border on parody, and even caricature. As though to enliven his stationary narrative, in the eighth chapter Roth has a distant Russian-Jewish relative of Perlefter's, Leo Bidak, arrive in Europe from San Francisco with his six children, and from then on his story fully eclipses that of the main figure. The last chapter hints that henceforth the two stories may somehow intertwine, but it ends after two short paragraphs.

With his novels *Hotel Savoy* and *Rebellion,* Roth had established himself in the eyes of critics as a budding writer whose career bore watching. By the end of the twenties and his—however ambiguous—period of New Objectivism, he had published another three novels in book form, and he had solidified his reputation as a journalist of the first order. Throughout this time, the general tenor of his critical reception remained fairly constant: As a novelist, he was seen as a representative of the young wartime generation, a sharp, unsentimental recorder of the social injustices of the postwar era. At the same time, however, little attention was paid to the political implications of his writing even though, in one form or another, in each of his novels Roth rejected the materialistic, profit-driven values of western European middle-class society.[17] While he himself reacted with irritation to what he saw as the artistic misperceptions of his work, he was still more disappointed by his lack of monetary success. Indeed, an especially cruel blow of fate had made him more dependent than ever on increased income from his books. In 1928, Friederike, his young wife, showed the first acute signs of the schizophrenia that eventually led to her fearful end in 1940 as a victim of Nazi euthanasia. At first hopeful that her condition could be restored to normal, Roth fell into despair after numerous setbacks. In a letter of 20 January 1930 to his writer-friend René Schickele, he conveyed his unhappiness: "Ten years of my marriage with this outcome have been like forty to me, and my natural inclination to grow old beyond my years worsens my external misfortune in a terrible way. Until now eight books, more than 1000 articles, for ten years ten hours of work every day, and today, when I am losing my hair, my teeth, my sexual potency, the most basic ability to feel happiness, I am not even in the position to live a single month without financial worries" (*BR* 156).

Friederike's misfortune was not to be overcome, and Roth remained psychologically tormented and financially burdened by it for the rest of his life. At this time, however, during which Roth was working on the never-completed *Perlefter* text, plausibly in 1929–1930, he had already begun writing his next novel, *Hiob* (*Job*), and it ushered in a new, artistically heightened phase of his career.

# CHAPTER 4

# The Pinnacle Years, 1930–1932

## The Jewish and Austrian Themes

### *Job*

In 1930, with *Hiob: Roman eines einfachen Mannes,* Roth gained his first major and enduring success as a fiction writer. A year later the novel appeared in English, translated by the American journalist-author Dorothy Thompson. Her repute as a foreign correspondent and later widely syndicated news columnist most likely contributed to the novel's selection by the Book-of-the-Month Club that November.[1] Underscoring Roth's break with the pessimism of postwar fiction, the poet and anthologist Louis Untermeyer wrote in the influential *Saturday Review of Literature* that the choice of *Job* by the book club "signifies, without proclaiming the fact, that the chronicling of emotion—downright and self-declared emotion—has lost none of its potency" (*KAT* 445).

In *Job* Roth abandoned the broad social and political criticism of New Objectivism that typified his earlier work. Instead, he granted primacy to the sorrows and triumphs of the human heart. While the fate he portrayed in the novel was distinctly individual in its ethnic-religious contours and coloring, as a modern-day Job legend it was also universal in its human appeal. In place of the lost generation of World War I veterans and their search for personal fulfillment, as personified by Franz Tunda, Paul Bernheim, and Arnold Zipper, he related the story of a lowly Russian Jew, Mendel Singer, who is barely able to support his wife and children by instructing children in the Bible, and—like Andreas Pum in *Rebellion*—comes to despair of divine justice and rebel against God. With that, Roth transferred the setting of his novel from the capitals of political unrest in central and western Europe to the everyday world of the shtetl, the east European Jewish town familiar to him from his childhood and youth in Galicia; and in keeping with the shift in thematic focus, he turned definitively from the analytic, eyewitness style popularized by New Objectivism to the lyricism and inner subjectivity that henceforth were to be lauded as distinctive features of his novels and stories.

The introductory lines of *Job* signal that Roth conceived of his "children's teacher," Mendel Singer, as an antipode to the starkly secularized protagonists of the three novels that preceded it. Without the supportive belief in a higher moral order, these sought restlessly and, in the end, futilely for the place in the sun that their fathers' generation denied them. Singer, on the other hand, lives a life whose very commonplaceness would appear to exclude the conflicts of personal freedom and social identity that typified Roth's returnees to their prewar homes. Roth says of Singer: "He was pious, God-fearing and ordinary, an entirely commonplace Jew. . . . He taught with honorable zeal and without notable success. Hundreds of thousands before him had lived and taught as he did" (*J* 3). Despite his humble calling as a *Kinderlehrer,* or "children's teacher," (Roth's approximation of the Hebrew-Yiddish *melamed*), Singer himself knows that his life is embedded in a tradition that gives it discernible shape and form. As the immigration of his family to America approaches, he reflects: "My father was teacher here, and my grandfather; and here I, too, was a teacher. Now I am going to America" (*J* 110). Along with the melancholy of departure and uncertainty of the future, there pulsates in his words the self-reproach that he is uprooting himself from a life that binds him to the spiritual legacy and traditions of his forebears.

The afflictions that befall Singer both in Russia and America—the sickness and death that gradually destroy his family—are known to humankind universally. Yet, Roth casts them in a mold that is intrinsically Jewish. In itself, certainly, Singer's chance discovery that his daughter, Miriam, has been promiscuously gratifying her sexual desire would suffice to alarm the family. What impels the Singers's departure from Zuchnow and Russia, however, is the still more unsettling fact that she sates her forbidden lust with the gentile soldiers of the nearby garrison, or, as Singer calls them with a mix of contempt and dread, "cossacks." Indeed, his horror that "Miriam is going with a Cossack" expresses more than just the plight of a single Jewish family (*J* 82). In the most succinct form, it reflects the generations-old collective Jewish memory in Russia and Poland of the catastrophic Chmielnicki massacres of 1648, and the utter rejection of all that could be associated with them.[2] Compounding Singer's pain, the younger and more robust of his sons, Jonas, espouses the earthy ways of the Russian peasants around them. Drinking and sleeping with the peasant girls, he alienates himself from his family and the Jewish world of Zuchnow. Voluntarily, he joins the czar's army and thus lives by choice beyond the pale of Jewish law and custom. Singer's older son, Shemariah, who has preceded the family to America in order to avoid military service (and later dies as an American soldier in the First World War), there discards the traditional garb of the Orthodox Jew as well as his given Hebrew name. As Sam Singer, in an uncertain yet palpable way, as Mendel himself recognizes, he has ceased to be his father's son. Menuchim, the youngest son, believed to be incurably retarded from his earliest years, is left behind in Zuchnow—despite the stricture of the rabbi to whom his mother had journeyed in her distress not to abandon the child. Lacking news of Menuchim during the years of war and turmoil in Russia, the family assumes that he has perished there. Thus, Singer grieves by the body of his wife, Deborah, who has died of heartbreak in New York on learning of Shemariah's fate: "It is only sad that you have no son left to mourn you. I myself must say the prayer for the dead; but I will soon die, and no one will weep for us" (*J* 169).

The key to understanding the Jewish ethos inherent in Singer's lament lies in the mourner's prayer, the *kaddish*. Upon the repeated sanctification of God's name, the prayer, which is concerned with neither death nor mourning, concludes with the wish for life and peace for all of Israel. It has been described as a "handclasp between the generations" and, in Yiddish-speaking families, *meyn kaddish* has served as a common term of endearment for a son, on whom it would fall to intone the prayer after a parent's death.[3] Significantly, the prayer may not be recited privately, but only in a quorum of fellow Jews; for Israel is seen to embrace every Jew, vertically through history and horizontally in the community of the living. Martin Buber writes of this relationship of the individual Jew to the Jewish people, suggesting that they are linked together at a point marked in eternity in a great chain of generations. "The past of his people," he says, "is his personal memory; the future of his people is his personal task."[4] The sorrow of Mendel Singer that no son will remain after him to recite the *kaddish* is grounded not in anxiety for his soul's redemption, of which there is mention neither in the prayer itself nor in the novel, but in the unspoken concern that the last bond of his family to its past and the House of Israel has been severed. More profoundly than milieu and setting, this religious ethos of generational continuity, remembrance, and Jewish peoplehood supports the widely held view of *Job* as a key work of what has been called the German-Jewish literary symbiosis, and of Joseph Roth as one of its prime representatives.[5]

It is this same vision of transcendent historical connectedness that lends the "miracle" in which Roth's Job story culminates its particular Jewish significance and, in general, a dimension of meaning that is absent altogether in the thoroughly profane novels of New Objectivism that preceded *Job*. The return to Mendel of his now-renowned musician son, Menuchim, long believed dead, restores the broken chain of generations in the Singer family. Implicit in Mendel's joy at the miracle of his son's return is a renewed faith in the continuity of life and the eternal link between the living and the departed. Through the miracle, as Mendel's immigrant neighbors urge him to see, he is united at heart with his dead wife, Deborah, whose girlhood features he discerns in a photograph of his son's wife; and, through Menuchim's children, he is reunited spiritually with his own children

Miriam and Jonas. Bolstered by these signs of God's justice, he now has the faith to believe in Menuchim's promise that Miriam will be cured of her mental illness and Jonas will return safely from the war.

That Menuchim was cured in a Russian hospital through the "gentile" medical science Mendel had once rejected, and that he will seek similar profane help for his sister should, it would seem, awaken Mendel to dimensions of faith less restrictive than those that underlay his helplessness in the face of sickness and loss. However, he accepts the "miracle" without question. More than the dramatic nature of the novel's conclusion, which has been criticized as contrived, as a Hollywood ending, it is this failure of insight and personal vision on Mendel's part that strains Roth's biblical analogy.

The tragic flaw in Mendel Singer's life lies, ironically, in his fidelity to God's word, which earlier had sustained him in an encompassing sense—on the one hand as the goods of his meager livelihood as a children's Bible teacher, and on the other as the law that regulated his life from daybreak to nightfall. His retort to Deborah, as she contrives to have their two elder sons smuggled abroad in order to escape military service during Russia's war with Japan, encapsulates Singer's unquestioning obedience to what he views as divine will: "Let each suffer his lot! Let the sons serve, they won't go to the bad; against the will of heaven there is no power. 'He is the thunder and the lightning, He arches himself above the whole world, no man can escape Him,' thus it is written" (*J* 45). His resolute, practical wife, who remonstrates that God helps those who help themselves, is unable to prevail against Singer's surrender to hostile circumstance. Tragic though it may be, Singer can only cleave to the Word as he all too literally comprehends it. Thus he submits passively to misfortune. And because he can discover no transgression against this Word in himself, the further misfortunes that he experiences in America appear to him all the more cruel and unjust.

Mendel Singer's rebellion against God erupts only when the blows of fate that strike his house mount beyond his endurance. It arises from the despair of a simple believer whose life had been grounded in the covenantal understanding that God punishes the guilty but hears the supplications of the just. When he sees this belief negated in devastating form, and finds no answer within himself or in the world about him to the existential question "Why me?," he refuses God the obedience that had been the hallmark of his faith. He rails against God and refuses to pray, even on the eve of Yom Kippur, the holiest day of the Jewish year. In Roth's unfolding of the Job analogy, however, the misfortunes that befall Singer are not shown to be the trials of faith to which an inscrutable deity subjects the unswerving believer. Rather, they represent the senseless calamities of existence in a world that is no longer governed by a divine order, but open on all sides to the forces of secularity. Believing that he had been punished unjustly by

God, Singer succumbs to despair—much as his determined wife, Deborah, had finally forsaken hope as she struggled to save their afflicted son Menuchim. "But the strength which belongs with faith," the narrator comments, "was no longer hers, and gradually she was losing the strength which is needed to endure despair" (*J* 114).

For Mendel Singer to withstand his crisis of faith he required the "miracle" of Menuchim's return. Yet Roth also reveals in him a purely ethical impulse that transcends the religious specificity of "this most Jewish of [his] novels," as it has been rightly described (*DB* 382). Although Singer's losses have exceeded all bearable measure, he finds the strength to search within himself for his failings. In mute conversation with his dead wife, he attains an insight into the tragedy of his life that the stubborn literalness of his belief had always hidden from him: "Because the warmth of love was not in us," he reflects, "but only the frost of familiarity, everything around us perished, or was ruined" (*J* 169). Self-knowledge of this kind, however, is ill-suited to reconcile Mendel Singer with his fate. On the contrary, to accept its moral verdict would overcome him with guilt. Nonetheless, the unalloyed humanity that imbues this act of recognition rests sovereignly in itself, undiminished and untainted by Singer's adversity. Although he will quarrel with God because of God's cruelty, his inner searching transforms what might be the reader's pity for an uncomprehending sufferer into sympathetic admiration, and lends the pathos of the novel's conclusion, which continues to exercise and divide Roth's commentators, its own redeeming dignity.

Roth, however, was unable to weather the crisis of his personal life that inspired him to write the novel: the tragic illness of his wife, Friederike. As his efforts to find help for her grew desperate—like Deborah in *Job,* he sought the counsel of a Hassidic rabbi living in Berlin—his guilt at having neglected his young bride intensified. To fight off his depression and, as he protested to concerned friends, in order to write, he drank more and more. Buffeted by his misfortune and, despite generous monthly payments from his publisher Kiepenheuer, ever more strained financially, he despaired of hope and a tolerable future. In letters from this period to Friederike's family and friends he described himself as a sufferer in the image of Job. "A curse has struck me," he wrote to Friederike's mother, "only God can help."[6] And in the same letter: "The dear Lord is punishing us, who knows for what."[7] In still another, he declared to her: "I'm finished with life, for good. I can no longer wait, not for miracles. I've become an old man and have grown used to feeling no joy" (*BR* 185). That Roth reflected these and similar emotions in the figure of Mendel Singer and incorporated in Singer's daughter, Miriam, features of his stricken wife, Friederike, underscores the cathartic function that he had doubtlessly hoped his new book would fulfill.

Given its geographical locale and ethnic-religious ambiance, Roth's *Job* can be legitimately placed amid the large body of fiction, written mainly in Yiddish, but also in German, that is set in the world of east European Jewry. In this connection, one thinks above all of the books of the classic Yiddish authors Mendele Mokher Sforim (1835–1917), Sholem Aleichem (1859–1916), and Isaac Leib Peretz (1852–1915). Commonly referred to as "shtetl literature," this genre found its most profiled German-language representative in Emil Franzos (1848–1904), who was like Roth an Austrian and native of Galicia.[8] What particularly relates *Job* to such works is Roth's depiction, in the fate of Mendel Singer, of the dissolution of traditional shtetl values as European modernity made its inroads. Despite their relatively late arrival among east Europe's Jews, the liberal outlooks of modernity were threatening to break up a folk culture anchored for centuries in religious law and rabbinic authority. In one way or another, each of Singer's four children illustrates this process. They follow the allurements of the alien modern world beyond the confines of the shtetl, both in Russia and—in the novel's second half—in America, and directly or indirectly they succumb to them.

Seen in this light, it may be argued that as a novel *Job* would have been more compelling had Roth substantially emphasized the theme of assimilation, which as a subtext plays a key role in Singer's tribulations. But such emphasis would have required Roth to harmonize the novel's lyric character with its sociology, something that ran counter to his intent when he set about to write the "story of a simple man" in the mold of a contemporary Job legend. Seen against the background of Roth's own assimilation, however, *Job* may indicate that it was less than a full and altogether persuasive one. On the contrary, in writing his novel about the *Ostjude* Mendel Singer, set in a Russian shtetl and the Jewish tenement world of New York, to an uncertain yet palpable degree Roth himself placed in question the assimilation he had achieved to that point as a self-chosen Austrian and a German writer. Seemingly, he had left behind his Galician-Jewish origins and upbringing in far-off Brody, but, faced with an extreme trial in his personal life, it appears that he felt driven to express himself Jewishly. With that, however, he hyphenated himself; and as a German-Jewish author he wrote the novel that Jewish tradition and faith gave him to write—with all of the tensions of identity that the problematic label implies.

Thematically, as a novel of Jewish existence, *Job* marks a turning point in Roth's development. At the same time, however, it occupies a unique place within the body of his fictional work. Although he continued to integrate significant motifs from Jewish and particularly east European Jewish life into his novels and stories, only in *Job* did he shape and fuse them so thoroughly and with such paradigmatic purpose.

## The Radetzky March

If *Job* may be seen as an affirmation of Roth's ties to his Jewish heritage, *The Radetzky March* may be regarded as his declaration of faith as an Austrian. In an often-cited letter of 28 October 1932 to the Austrian literary historian Otto Forst de Battaglia, Roth stated: "My most unforgettable experience was the war and the end of my fatherland, *the only one* that I have ever had: the Austro-Hungarian monarchy" (*BR* 240). In the same year, the author's literary tribute to this home-land, *The Radetzky March,* first appeared as a serialized preprint in the *Frank-furter Zeitung,* and then in book form. In his foreword to the newspaper version of the novel, Roth declared the following: "The cruel will of history destroyed my old fatherland, the Austro-Hungarian Monarchy. I loved this fatherland. It permitted me to be a patriot and a citizen of the world at the same time, among all the Austrian peoples also a German. I loved the virtues and merits of this fatherland, and today, when it is dead and gone, I even love its flaws and weak-nesses" (*W* 4: 405).

The fact that Roth set to writing *The Radetzky March* in the early 1930s is indicative of the historical consciousness of those Austrian generations, both older and younger, who had grown to maturity before World War 1. In 1918 they witnessed the dissolution of the monarchy and then the precariousness of the diminished and embattled First Republic that succeeded it. The new Austria suf-fered economic want and political discord; it lacked both a clearly defined iden-tity and the broad popular support vital to a national existence. Increasingly, it was rent by civil strife, and the paramilitary groups of the Socialist left and the Christian-Social right stood ready for armed struggle. When Hitler took power in Germany, violent agitation by the illegal Nazi party mounted. In March 1933 the new chancellor, Engelbert Dollfuss, suspended parliamentary government and less than a year later proscribed all parties except his own fascist Fatherland Front. In the civil war that ensued, the Social Democratic party was destroyed, and in April 1934 Dollfuss assumed dictatorial rule.

These turbulent events, along with the looming threat from Nazi Germany to the country's independence, caused many Austrians, belatedly, to feel the loss of the monarchy as a profoundly personal one. Like Roth, other writers, some of them long since prominent, felt the need to preserve in literature what Stefan Zweig called in the title of his memoirs, "the world of yesterday."[9] In 1930, Robert Musil published the first part of his monumental novel *The Man without Qualities* (1930–1943); in his drama *3. November 1918* (1936), Franz Theodor Csokor (1885–1969) portrayed the final days of Habsburg Austria; in 1937 the Prague-born Franz Werfel (1890–1945) gathered eight of his Old Austrian sto-ries and short novels in the collection *Twilight of a World,* for which he wrote a glowing tributary prologue, "An Essay upon the Meaning of Imperial Austria."[10] At its conclusion, Werfel declared: "Austria was a wonderful home, a home of humanity without regard to blood or confession, to origin or goal of its children. The Austrian born in old Austria has no longer a home."[11] Werfel's last words ring like an echo of the poet Hofmannsthal's declaration in a letter of 1928 to the historian Josef Redlich that when Austria collapsed he lost the ground in which he was rooted.[12] Like Roth, both Werfel and Hofmannsthal had once been critical of the monarchy, but, again like Roth, in their reflections they endowed it with an aura that arose far more from wish than from reality.

The feeling of loss, however, was real, and what sharpened it most acutely was the growing menace from Nazi Germany. Above all for the Jews of Austria, the danger was a mortal one. Even before the Nuremberg racial laws were issued in the Third Reich in 1935, Roth was forced to recognize that the assimilation he had so aimfully pursued was tenuous. In the face of a racist ideology that was soon to make pariahs of others still better known than he, the newly successful author was fated once more to become an outsider. Disabused of any claim to the German identity with which he had ambiguously flirted as late as 1931 and to which he alludes in his foreword to *The Radetzky March,* he also found that he had lost his foothold in Austria.[13] He acknowledged to his friend Stefan Zweig in September 1934: "Since Hitler, the Austrian papers treat me as though I do not exist. I no longer have any friends in the editorial offices" (*BR* 381).

After 1933, Roth repeated and varied the essential motifs of his foreword in the essays and articles that he penned for various émigré journals. Taken together, these declarations show how the exiled author abandoned the critical view of Habsburg Austria and the First Republic that he had espoused during the early postwar years, and began more and more to extol the monarchy as a lost paradise. He did this despite the fact that he had grown to young manhood far from the deceptive splendor of Vienna, the capital he had gotten to know for only a brief time before the outbreak of the First World War. In contrast to Vienna, where the aura of the royal court might still nurture illusions of Habsburg might, Roth's native Galicia was rife with the national tensions that would soon bring about Austria's fall.

Among the episodes in *The Radetzky March* that, when viewed together, most strikingly convey this dissonance of appearance and reality are those of the traditional Imperial Corpus Christi procession in Vienna and an open-air regimental officers fête in the distant Galician province where his young protagonist is stationed. In the one, the grandeur of the empire is lavishly celebrated as though Austria's glories were destined to endure forever; in the other, the regimental celebration is first disrupted by a thunder storm, and then, upon the news that the heir to the throne has been shot, it degenerates into a danse macabre of drunken officers, gloatingly led by nationalist Hungarians, that sounds the doom of the empire. This contrast of scenes drives home the idea that in the border-lands of the monarchy seductive escape from the illusions nurtured in Vienna was impossible. The Galician Roth knew this and portrayed it masterfully, yet he also embraced the illusions as though they, rather than the dark reality they hid, represented the substance of his own experience. Far more than the demise of Old Austria, it was the political circumstances of the early 1930s, along with the calamities of his personal life, that led Roth to take flight from the present and seek solace in a subjectively transfigured past.

The historical understanding that lay beneath this turn in Roth's outlook from his earlier, negative one was metaphysically determined, and it grew still more pronounced during the author's exile years. Despite the verdict of history, the proponents of this view persisted in regarding Habsburg Austria as a divinely ordained hierarchical entity, as the living heir to the Holy Roman Empire of the German Nation, the center of which it had once formed. For Joseph Roth, Austrian universality was an article of faith. Thus, the monarchy was fated to decline when its constituent peoples betrayed the principle of supranationality for what Roth condemned quite literally as the idolatry of nationalism. "Austria," he was later to write in his novel *The Emperor's Tomb* (1938), "is neither a state, a home nor a nation. It is a religion" (*ET* 145). In *The Radetzky March* it is the Galician-Polish landowner Count Chojnicki, portrayed as the embodiment of Austrianism, who voices this conviction, clearly in Roth's own name:

> People no longer believe in God. The new religion is nationalism. Nations no longer go to church. They go to national associations. Monarchy, our monarchy, is founded on piety, on the faith that God chose the Habsburgs to rule over so and so many Christian nations. Our Kaiser is a secular brother of the Pope, he is His Imperial and Royal Apostolic Majesty; no other is as apostolic, no other majesty in Europe is as dependent on the grace of God and the faith of the nations in the grace of God. . . . The Emperor of Austria-Hungary must not be abandoned by God. But God *has* abandoned him![14]

Emperor Franz Joseph—along with the "Radetzky March" itself and the por-trait of the Hero of Solferino, the grandfather of the protagonist, Carl Joseph von Trotta—is a prime symbol of the novel. He appears in person or image whenever Roth wishes to exemplify the hierarchical essence of Habsburg Austria and fore-shadow Austria's disintegration. Roth portrays him with both his virtues and fail-ings: the acquired wisdom and dignity of his old age as well as his whimsicality and forgetfulness.[15] However ironically Roth may sometimes depict the emperor, however, his filial affection for him—a lofty surrogate figure for the father he never knew—remains steady. In his poetic "Rede über den alten Kaiser" (Speech on the Old Emperor) of 1938, the year Nazi Germany annexed Austria, he wrote: "Our father is Franz Joseph the First" (*W* 4:772).

To the degree that Roth's story of the Trottas, a Slovenian peasant family ennobled by the emperor two generations earlier, authentically mirrors the crisis and end of the Habsburg monarchy, *The Radetzky March* qualifies as a historical novel. It would be false, however, to regard Roth's generational tale of a family's rise and decline as a vehicle for narrating history. Indeed, as some contemporary critics objected, he conspicuously avoided unfolding in the novel the concrete social and political developments that brought about the collapse of the empire.[16] Rather, in the personal tragedy of his central figure and the last member of the family, Carl Joseph von Trotta, Roth created a microcosm of the larger historical event. In the story of the anxious, guilt-laden young officer Trotta, helplessly entangled in his own memories, fears, and longings, Roth reflected the dissolution of Imperial Austria in an individually sublimated form. In both instances, that of the family Trotta and of the empire, the decline was determined by a loss of faith in the sustaining creed of Austrian universality.

For Trotta's grandfather, the legendary Hero of Solferino, Austria had been a boundless homeland—in his eyes "the entire world"—and Franz Joseph I its personification. As an infantry lieutenant he had risked his life to save the young emperor from an enemy bullet, a deed that won the family lasting imperial favor. For Trotta's father, an early widower, habitually reserved and distant, even from his only child, this vision of Austria as the vast, inviolable realm of the emperor Franz Joseph remained intact—above all because he was careful never to reflect on it. Denied a military career by paternal decree, he punctiliously fulfills the family mission of service to the monarchy as a district commissioner in provincial Moravia. Despite his utter lack of imagination, in his loyalty to the crown Trotta embodies the very ideal of Habsburg officialdom. Franz Werfel could just as well have had him before his eyes when in his novel *Der Abituriententag* (1928; Class Reunion), he described the Prague Latin teacher Kio as "the epitome of the Old Austrian man and official":

> Without serving, or even belonging to, a single people or class, this Kio, this Old Austrian, was filled with the lofty dignity of a hierarchy, that transcended all that was personal, that tolerated no national arrogance. . . .
>
> The state was sacred, a higher world, heaven, as it were, that had secretly descended to earth in order to deliver it from sin.
>
> The highest official was God.

But God was an invisible authority, who could be reached only indirectly through an ascending order of official channels, with the help of the lower and higher clergy.

God wore neither a civil service nor a military uniform. As His next in rank, his Royal-and-Imperial Apostolic Majesty, the emperor in Vienna, wore a general's uniform with oak leaves on the collar to distinguish him from the other generals.

From the emperor the ladder descended unbroken to the bottom rung, on which stood the first form of a Royal-Imperial State Gymnasium.[17]

Like Werfel's Kio, who chafes at "the subversive elements" within the state,[18] Roth's Trotta is upset by reports of the disloyal "national minorities" and faceless "revolutionary individuals" and their agents in the army (*RM* 228). But until he is rudely awakened from his political naiveté, he fails to discern the stirrings of political dissent as irreversible symptoms of Austria's nearing end. His son, however, a melancholy, touchingly inept cavalry officer, mirrors this decline in his own person.

Unlike his father, the exemplary civil servant, Carl Joseph experiences his life as empty and aimless. Burdened from his youth by the heroic legend of his grandfather, he suffers from a sense of superfluousness as a career soldier without a war. His existence is governed by a feeling of inescapable doom, from which he finds only momentary refuge in drink, gambling, and amorous interludes in Vienna. In contrast to both his father and grandfather, he seeks vainly to discover an Austria that might offer him a true homeland, one in which he could meaningfully anchor his unfulfilled life. For him, Austria exists solely in memories of his grandfather's fading portrait in the Moravian home of his boyhood and the strains of the "Radetzky March," played there each Sunday by a military band. As the last of his lineage, he manages only pathetically to emulate the heroic feat of his grandfather: during a reluctant visit to a brothel with his carousing comrades, he rescues a portrait of the emperor from the brothel wall.

Carl Joseph's petition to be transferred to an infantry unit in Slovenia after the death of his sole friend, the Jewish regimental surgeon Max Demant, reflects his desire to be united with the Hero of Solferino, whose own father had originated in the Slovenian village of Sipolje. "His grandfather," he reflects, "had likewise been a simple infantry captain. Marching across his native soil would almost mean coming home to his peasant forbears" (*RM* 115). What Carl Joseph fails to realize, however, is that, through ennoblement, his grandfather himself had been cut off from the family's Slovenian past. When the Hero of Solferino visits his father, Carl Joseph's great-grandfather, he perceives how the splendor of his captain's uniform, the newly bestowed Order of Maria Theresa, and his title of nobility now separate the two of them. Although he understands little Slovenian, he awaits a greeting in this language—in the hope that it will restore their lost closeness. When the old man, himself a war veteran, congratulates him in German, the Hero of Solferino knows that the gulf between them is unbridgeable: "Captain Trotta," Roth's narrator comments, "was severed from the long procession of his Slavic peasant forebears. A new dynasty began with him" (*RM* 6). Unbeknown to Carl Joseph, his romantic wish to serve the military in Slovenia betrays the longing for a homeland that lies historically beyond Austria. As a personalized variant of the same nationalism that menaces Austria from within, it negates the Austrian principle of supranationality.

By contrast, Roth depicts in another Austrian military family, likewise of Slavic descent, an entirely concrete instance of the national strivings that spelled the end of the monarchy. In an inner monologue, the Slovene *rittmaster* Jelacich meditates: "For some hundred and fifty years his family had been serving the Habsburgs with sincerity and devotion. But both his teenage sons were already talking about independence for all southern Slavs, and they had pamphlets that they concealed from him—pamphlets that might come from a hostile Belgrade. . . . He was intelligent and he knew that he stood powerless between his forebears and his offspring, who were destined to become ancestors for a brand-new race" (*RM* 297). For his part, the district commissioner senses in his son's request for transfer the more immediate threat to the assimilation of his family as Austrians that had been achieved only a generation earlier by the Hero of Solferino. Thus, he admonishes Carl Joseph: "Fate has turned our family of frontier peasants into an Austrian dynasty. That is what we shall remain" (*RM* 126).

Transferred to a rifle battalion in Galicia, which he wistfully regards as the "northern sister" of Slovenia, Carl Joseph soon succumbs to the hazards of army life in the oppressively dreary border province. Increasingly, he turns to alcohol and gambling in order to flee his forlornness. Alongside the debt he incurs with the ruthless casino owner Kapturak, he performs his duties carelessly, neglects his appearance, and damages his health. "Any stranger coming into this region," Roth's narrator observes, "was doomed to gradual decay. No one was as strong as the swamp. No one could hold out against the borderland" (*RM* 129). Far from their homes, separated by custom and language from their environs, Carl Joseph's fellow officers have slowly yielded to the decadence of garrison life. Thanks to his overly sensitive nature, however, the young lieutenant's decline proceeds more quickly. Thus occurs the disquiet of the district commissioner when he visits his son at the frontier. In Carl Joseph's wasted young manhood the elder Trotta recognizes his helplessness as a father, in Carl Joseph's loneliness he sees his own loneliness. Only on the frontier does he realize that an unbridgeable distance separates him from his son, that the rituals and conventions he had employed lifelong in order to fulfill his role as an official and father no longer sufficed to save him from ruin. As much as Count Chojnicki's jarring prophecy of Austria's demise, Carl Joseph's condition, symbolic of that of the army itself, awakens the elder Trotta to a new and, for him, mournful reality.

To the end, Carl Joseph seeks a return to the home and ways of his Slovenian ancestors. He eventually quits the military and lives among the Ukrainian peasants as an estate steward for Count Chojnicki. For a time he feels a measure of inner peace through this isolation, but his attempt to return "home" is cut short when the First World War breaks out. He rejoins his regiment in the illusory belief that at last "his war, a grandson's war," had arrived and he could now relive the glory of the Hero of Solferino. Instead he falls in a rain of bullets while selflessly but rashly fetching water for his troops. In dying, he attempts to answer in Ukrainian to the peasants of his platoon who call out in chorus: "Praised be Jesus Christ" (*RM* 320). But before he can complete the doxology through his own response, his lips are sealed. Thus he dies unfulfilled. In the end, even symbolically, he was unable to restore the bond with his legendary grandfather and his family's ethnic origins. Neither his pedantic, unresponsive father nor his elusive Austrian homeland nor the army—for other Roth figures their one secure, unquestioned haven—had been able to nourish his homeless existence.

This theme of the severed generational bond finds an eloquent parallel in the subplot of the friendship between the young Trotta and Dr. Max Demant, the surgeon of the cavalry regiment. Both are inept and unhappy as soldiers, both are isolated among their comrades. More essentially, however, they are bound in a brief friendship by the knowledge that each of them is heir to a tradition he is too weak to carry forward. Like Trotta, Demant is a grandson and is fated to be the last in his lineage. Like Trotta, too, he feels as though he lives off the dead. His grandfather inhabits his memories as a robust, silver-bearded Orthodox Jewish innkeeper in Galicia, who on the Sabbath devoted himself to his pious books. Demant's father had broken with family tradition after militia service by becoming a mid-level postal official, "an abomination to the old man, though he lovingly tolerated him" (*RM* 78). Demant himself had once hoped for a medical and university career, but his life had been, as he puts it, "a life with snags" (*RM* 77). Faced by a duel with a fellow officer over personal honor, which Trotta had indirectly and innocently provoked, Demant confesses to his friend: "Our grandfathers did not bequeath us great strength—little strength for life, it's just barely enough to die senselessly. . . . Tomorrow I'm going to die like a hero, a so-called hero, completely against my grain, and against the grain of my forebears and my tribe and against my grandfather's will. One of the huge old tomes he used to read says, 'He who raiseth his hand against his neighbor is a murderer'" (*RM* 102). In reverence to his grandfather, the near-sighted Demant decides that he will remove his glasses before the duel: "I will shoot without seeing. That will be more natural, more honest, and altogether fitting" (*RM* 102). As he departs for the dueling ground, he glances upward and hears from the sky, like "a distant echo from a distant childhood," the extinguished voice of his grandfather chanting the *sh'ma*, the Jewish declaration of faith to be recited in the face of death (*RM* 109). The great irony of the duel is that, inexplicably, Demant is able to see clearly without his glasses and, in dying, also kills his opponent. Thus, despite his resolve to honor the faith of his forebears, he appears to have trespassed against it. Roth's intention is unclear—perhaps purposely so in order to underscore the futility of Demant's life and the poignancy of its end. Yet, the thought is intriguing that Roth may have wished to grant to his Jewish doctor what he withheld from his Austrian lieutenant: to be a link, even if the last link, in the chain of generations that binds him through his family to his people.

By determining on a military career for Carl Joseph, the district commissioner Trotta had intended to carry on the Austrian tradition that for a moment in history his own father had gloriously represented. In the story of their relationship, Roth united the two major themes of his novel, the decline of a prototypical Austrian family and the collapse of the monarchy. Accompanying and intertwined with both is Roth's portrayal of the emperor, whose actual or felt presence pervades the novel. A reckless young man when saved by Carl Joseph's grandfather during the battle of Solferino, at the end he is as feeble as his threatened realm. But while the officers of his suite regard him with bemused tolerance, Roth grants him the self-knowledge and historical insight that rescue him in the reader's eye from the shame of decrepitude. Franz Joseph knows well that in an epoch of nationalism his reign is irreversibly nearing its end, and he accepts this decree of history with a disarmingly simple dignity: "They just don't want to be ruled by me anymore! thought the old man. What can you do? he added to himself. For he was an Austrian" (*RM* 225).

In the final chapter of the novel, titled "Epilogue," the district commissioner Trotta, still mourning the war death of his son, dies on the same day as his emperor, Franz Joseph. On this confluence of events, the physician Dr. Skowronnek remarks to the mayor of W., the Trottas's provincial home: "I don't think either of them could have outlived Austria" (*RM* 331). Two years later, with the end of World War I, history wrote its own epilogue to Roth's novel. In their quest for national independence, the peoples of the monarchy created the new geographical and political borders that dissolved the Austria of Franz Joseph. Two generations of the Trottas had served it with undivided allegiance, but for the family's last member Austria had ceased to exist as an authentic homeland. In his own search for a rooted existence, Carl Joseph, unawares, broke the new covenant of faith into which the emperor had taken his family through its ennoblement. Whereas his father, like the emperor Franz Joseph, died along with Austria, at some indeterminate point in his young life the idea of Austria had died within him.

More lastingly than any other German-language writer, Joseph Roth memorialized two national communities, the Austrians under Habsburg and the Jews of eastern Europe—among whom those of the Austrian borderlands must be counted. The novels *Job* and *The Radetzky March* endure as their literary monuments, and each also marks an important turning point not only within Roth's literary work but also in his life. Driven by grief over his wife's devastating illness, in 1930 Roth had sought to mirror in *Job*—his "most Jewish" novel—the trials of faith tested and their ultimate reward. At that time, the world of his protagonist Mendel Singer, which had once also been his, still existed. Little could he know that it would soon be destroyed without a trace, and that his book would become a memorial to it. Two years later, in *The Radetzky March,* he turned to his second great theme. For the first time he depicted the world of Habsburg Austria, which had already sunken into history before he could genuinely claim it as his own. But what was denied him in life, the undisputed entry into the Austro-German cultural community, he attained as a writer. Critically but lovingly, in his novel he resurrected this world as a utopian vision of what might have been had the faith in Old Austria's constitutive ideal been stronger than the forces that led to its dissolution. His personal dilemma, however, remained and grew ever more acute while he was in exile. It lay in the impossibility of joining within himself the two identities, Austrian and Jewish, which express themselves in his two most famous works. In trying to secure the one, the Austrian, he seemingly felt himself compelled to deny the other, the Jewish, and of necessity he failed at both attempts. Even as his professions of Catholicism, which he equated with Austrianism, grew more ardent, he continued to see himself as a Jew from the eastern shtetl.

As both literary and biographical testimonies, *Job* and *The Radetzky March* must be regarded separately. The scene of *Job* in itself, with its motifs specific to Russian-Jewish life and history, sets the two novels distinctly apart—despite the strong Galician coloring in *The Radetzky March.* Yet, in this supremely Austrian work, Roth intuitively came profoundly close to revealing an essential affinity between the Austrian and the Jewish ethos reflected in the two books. Awaiting the duel that he knows is senseless, Max Demant confides to his younger friend Trotta: "You are the grandson of the Hero of Solferino. He almost died as senselessly. Though it does make a difference whether you go to your death with his deep faith or as faintheartedly as we two" (*RM* 102). The import of these words can only be inferred. It lies in the nature of the faith that Demant says he and Trotta lack. What Demant implies, it would seem, is the faith in a covenantal community, which Austria and the House of Israel constituted respectively for their forbears. In Demant's case, the chain of generations that binds him with this community extends back into history to the revelation at Sinai— as Martin Buber elucidates upon in his Stuttgart address of 1933. Through the ennoblement of the Hero of Solferino, the Trottas, too, had been taken by the emperor into a new covenant. It bore the name of Austria, and the tirade of Count Chojnicki against the idolatry of nationalism leaves no doubt that it was to be understood as a religious covenant. Only two generations later, the faith of the grandfathers had lost its power in the hearts of the grandsons. Although Demant acknowledges the sacred tradition against which he will trespass in the duel and attempts symbolically to restore his bond with it, he indeed dies senselessly; and the unfulfilled life of Carl Joseph von Trotta, too, ends in a senseless death. As the last keepers of the faith of their forebears, there remain Roth's revered Emperor Franz Joseph, who stands for Austria, and his equally revered *Ostjuden*.

In a key episode of the novel, Roth depicts army maneuvers in Galicia during which Franz Joseph is met by a throng of black-clad village Jews led by a white-bearded patriarch bearing a Torah scroll. Lifting the scroll toward the emperor, the Jew recites the blessing that orthodox believers pronounce on seeing a sovereign, and adds:

"Blessed art thou. . . . Thou shalt not live to see the end of the world."

I know! thought Franz Joseph. He shook the old man's hand. He turned around. He mounted his white horse.

He trotted to the left over the hard clods of the autumnal fields, his suite behind him. The wind brought him the words that Captain Kaunitz said to the friend riding at his side: "I didn't understand a thing the Jew said."

The Kaiser turned in his saddle and said, "He was speaking only to me, my dear Kaunitz," and rode on. (*RM* 223)

The emperor says nothing to the Jew, but, thanks to an inner kinship, he has understood the message that his reign and realm are finite. The last heir to the Austrian universal ideal and the Jew who has blessed him are joined spiritually through their belief in a providential existence. In Roth's metaphysical perspective, the idea of Austria as a divinely willed, all-embracing home, which transcends the nation-state, corresponds to the Orthodox Jewish understanding of exile as the reality of a nationally unbounded, holy peoplehood.[19] That the Jew's blessing is dismissed as babble in the emperor's own suite signals that the sustaining faith of the empire has been fatefully weakened.

The "miracle" of *Job,* which restored Mendel Singer's trust in God's justice, was a necessary thematic ingredient of the modern-day legend that Roth had set out to write. It was also integral to the cathartic effect from the novel that the despairing Roth must have promised himself at that time. On the other hand, the historical character of *The Radetzky March* in itself ruled out a "miracle." Long before Roth conceived the work, the hostile forces of history had pronounced sentence on Habsburg Austria, and the one theme left to him was that of its deceptive glories and the throes of its last years. Thus his book became an elegy for a lost paradise, which had never existed in the way his longing for a rooted life led him to describe it. In its pages, his own inner conflicts are resolved in the twilight glow of a humane vision, to which he gave the name Austria. It was a vision that allowed the Jewish doctor Max Demant and the Austrian cavalry lieutenant Carl Joseph von Trotta to find brotherly spirits in one another, and that joined Emperor Franz Joseph in silent understanding with a Galician Orthodox Jew. At the end of the 1934 story "The Bust of the Emperor," which revives the key theme of Austrian universalism embodied in *The Radetzky March,* the rabbi of the once Austrian and now Polish village of Lopatyny walks alongside the Greek-Catholic and Roman-Catholic priests as they accompany a bust of Franz Joseph to its burial; the tavern keeper Solomon Piniowsky strides with them, "wearing a little round black cap upon his silver hair . . . and raised in his right hand the black and yellow flag with the double eagle" (BE 181–82). In this Old Austrian world of mutual brotherly respect, idealized in the name of human goodness, there was also a place for "the wanderer in flight toward a tragic end," Joseph Roth.

Roth's devotion to the emperor and monarchy, so memorably evidenced in *The Radetzky March,* later intensified to absolute veneration of the Habsburgs, with extravagant hopes for their return to rule in the threatened Austrian republic. Several of his many friends and fellow writers during his exile years in Paris have described his politically unrealistic, even bizarre, schemes, centered on the pretender to the crown, Otto von Habsburg, and the Catholic Church, to save Austria and Europe from Nazism. But their accounts have only deepened the enigma of Roth's personal development. The young journalist of socialist leanings in his Vienna and Berlin years had given way, seemingly without transition, to the ardent, finally despairing monarchist-conservative, self-proclaimed Catholic, and equally avowed *Ostjude,* of the years after 1933.

# CHAPTER 5

# The Exile Years, 1933–1937

## The Novels of Guilt and Repentance

### *Tarabas*

Roth's first novel to appear in exile was the balladesque tale of sin and expiation, *Tarabas: Ein Gast auf dieser Erde* (1934; Tarabas: A Guest on Earth). Its title figure, like Franz Tunda of *Flight without End* before him, is a wanderer, a man without a home or binding personal ties. The subtitle calls him a "guest on earth," and at the story's end this epithet finds lasting expression on his gravestone. The inscription reminds the chance visitor to the gravesite of the transitoriness of earthly existence, and the words with which the Jewish innkeeper Nathan Kristianpoller concludes the novel echo this universal topos of human mortality: "[A]t the end of every life stands death. We all know it. And who remembers it?"[1] Applied to Nicholas Tarabas, the central protagonist, the epithet characterizes his varied encounters and relationships with key persons and places in the novel. With rare exceptions, they are transient and noncommittal. Tarabas was truly the "guest" who put down roots nowhere and was a stranger everywhere. When Kristianpoller says of him, years after the events depicted in the story, that he had been "a queer guest" in his inn, the local notary has only to add that he had been "a queer guest on earth altogether" in order to epitomize Tarabas's existence and therewith provide the inspiration for his epitaph (*T* 268).

While the plot of *Tarabas* begins in New York, the action of the last twenty-two of the novel's thirty chapters takes place in the small town of Koropta in an unnamed Russian border state populated by earthy peasants and simple yet discerning *Ostjuden*—the kinds of people, that is, with whom Roth had always felt a personal affinity. Twelve of these chapters are set either entirely or partially in Nathan Kristianpoller's inn, The White Eagle, where Tarabas, himself a Russian and commander of a new government military force, has taken quarters. It is here, at the start of the prominent Koropta section, that the most salient themes of the novel emerge. Closely interconnected, they can be described in terms of the antipodes evil and justness, rebellion and order, transience and continuity. For Tarabas, Kristianpoller's inn is a way station between his already half-forgotten past—as a rebellious son, a ne'er-do-well in New York (where he falsely believes that he killed a café owner), and as a rampaging officer during the Russian Revolution—and his precarious future, which had been foretold by a gypsy fortune teller in New York. She declared that Tarabas was "a murderer and a saint," who would "sin and atone—and both upon this earth" (*T* 8). Inasmuch as Tarabas himself accepted this prophecy as unalterable, it assumes decisive character for the course of his life. Seemingly, Roth wished to mirror this psychological state of affairs when he named part 1 of the novel "The Trial" and part 2 "Fulfillment." As a variant on this theme, Kristianpoller and the shopkeeper Nissen Pichenik reminisce at times on "the strange Colonel Tarabas, and how he came, a mighty king, into the little town, to be buried there a beggar" (*T* 271). Tarabas himself, however, neither recognizes the immorality of his violent actions nor can he foresee their consequences for his future life. Until the critical turning point in Koropta, his life constitutes a series of disconnected episodes.

In this sense, Kristianpoller's The White Eagle, through its very function as an inn, provides an emblematic setting for Tarabas's fragmentary, transient existence. On the other hand, The White Eagle assures Tarabas's unwilling host, Kristianpoller, the livelihood that sustains him and his family. Passed on to him through generations of his forbears, it also stands for tradition and continuity. Throughout the vicissitudes of the First World War and the Russian Revolution, Kristianpoller had succeeded in maintaining his life and that of his family at the inn. Upon Tarabas's arrival, however, his fate becomes dependent on the whims and wishes of the mighty and unpredictable regiment commander. At the same time, the encounter between the two men—one of whom embodies the principle of self-assertion through raw power, the other of self-preservation though inborn wit—sets off the decisive conflict of the main figure with his inner self. Tarabas's awakening from a life of brute instinct to remorse and repentance proceeds parallel to Kristianpoller's regaining of personal freedom after he has been robbed of it by his oppressive guest. This development reaches its decisive turning point when Tarabas, in the aftermath of a pogrom, abuses the feeble Jew Shemariah. Until that point, however, Tarabas's transformation from murderer to saint is reflected in his relationship to innkeeper Kristianpoller as it develops gradually during Tarabas's sojourn in Koropta.

Although, looking back, Kristianpoller calls the unwanted Tarabas a "guest" at his inn, Tarabas initially comes to Koropta as an occupier, who is all the more dangerous as he is legitimized by the state. From all others he expects unconditional obedience. In contrast to the commandeering Tarabas, Kristianpoller becomes a prisoner in his own home. For safety's sake, he sends his wife and their seven children to her parents in another town, and he gives up his own rooms for a straw mattress on the kitchen floor. What he could expect from Tarabas and his men he experiences on their first evening at the inn, which peaks in a tumult of drink and unleashed passions. Thus, Kristianpoller quickly realizes that in addition to house and home, his very life is at Tarabas's mercy, and as a Jew he is all the more vulnerable: "Motionless he stood beside his counter, a stranger in his own house. . . . All at a loss, miserable and busy despite his outward immobility, he stood there, the Jew Kristianpoller" (*T* 80).

Only as the unchallenged master of the house can the homeless Tarabas feel at peace with himself. Until his arrival in Koropta, he had, in fact, succeeded in determining events on his own. His sole defeats in life had come at the hands of his wrathful father, who twice banished him, the wayward son, from his home. In the war, however, he had found the opportunity to plunder and murder untrammeled, oblivious to the evil of his deeds. Now, as regiment commander, he attempts to carry over this same license into peacetime. Although he stands in the service of the new republic, he can only assert the autonomy that his violent nature demands beyond and in opposition to the laws of the state. For, to acknowledge these would mean to relinquish his own sovereignty. Thus, the forced recognition that he is no longer the master over life and death but rather a subject of the new government, and that he must answer to disgruntled superiors, threatens his existence as he has known it. Like Kristianpoller, he soon feels that he has lost the home, his sole one, that the army and war had been for him. Citing Tarabas's mounting unease over the government's demands for an orderly administration, the narrator registers his condition with critical empathy: "In the days that followed, Colonel Tarabas, the terrible king of Koropta, ceased to feel at home within his kingdom" (*T* 84).

At this point, Tarabas's fate crosses decisively with that of his victim Kristianpoller. Since the gypsy's prophesy has binding force for the thematic unfolding of the narrative, in order for Tarabas to become a "saint" he must first be humbled and brought to awareness of his sinful life. Only as the power to determine events steadily slips from Tarabas's hands can Kristianpoller, for his part, hope to regain his lost freedom. As this dialectic plays itself out, Kristianpoller's personal fate is transcended to symbolically reflect the historical plight of east European Jewry, an ethnic group periodically threatened with catastrophe because at any time it could falsely be charged with a bloodguilt it was helpless to deny.[2] That is, history itself, manifest in the collective consciousness of the Jews of Koropta and embodied by them, enters into the novel as a thematic element. Indeed, the historical significance with which the depicted events invest the novel supersedes the story of Nicholas Tarabas in a way that conspicuously disrupts the unity of the plot and creates a breach in its structure.

Thanks to an all but forgotten tale that, in times long past, a rickety lumber shed in the inn courtyard had been a Christian chapel, Kristianpoller must live with the fear that if the "secret" becomes known, he can be endangered at any time. Within the Koropta plot, Roth increasingly endows this motif of the supposedly desecrated chapel with a life of its own, and, finally, with great epic power, places it at the center of the pogrom episode in which Kristianpoller's misfortunes climax.

At the end of chapter 14, just as the innkeeper is thanking God for a peaceful and prosperous pig market in Koropta, the narrator confirms the inevitability of this misfortune: "But whilst the godly Kristianpoller marveled and gave praise, already the disaster was afoot, the great and bloody disaster of Koropta, and with it the dire aberration of the mighty Nicholas Tarabas" (T 118). What follows is the description of a pogrom from its inception to its aftermath, the madness and horror of which Roth depicted with profound psychological insight. That he attached prime value to this episode can be seen in the fact that it occupies almost the exact center of the novel, and that this fifteenth chapter, though it describes only half a day, is by far the longest in the book. The resultant disruption of narrative unity can be palpably felt. What more than compensates for it is the consummate artistry with which Roth portrayed the interlinked chapel and pogrom episodes.

The disaster that befalls the Jews of Koropta is set off by a deserter from Tarabas's regiment, the sinister Ramzin, who mysteriously knows the "secret" of the lumber shed. With satanic skill, before the eyes of Tarabas's loyal soldiers, a troop of deserters, and the peasants who had come to Koropta for the market, Ramzin creates a "miracle." By firing at lewd pictures he himself had drawn on the shed wall he exposes a plastered-over image of the Holy Virgin. The readiness of the peasants to believe in this "miracle" is nourished by their childlike piety, while the effects of a day of drinking sweep the soldiers into the same state of religious ardor. It takes only the murderous demagogy of Ramzin to turn the devotion of the transported crowd into rage against the hapless innkeeper, whom Ramzin has targeted as the desecrator of the chapel. But, almost at the same moment, their fury transforms into seething hatred for the Jews of Koropta collectively, as members of a despised and feared people: "The Jew!—The ancient specter, sown thousandfold in the length and breadth of all the land, the festering enemy in the flesh, incomprehensible, nimble-witted, gentle and yet bloodthirsty, cruel and yielding, more frightful than all the frightfulness of the war that they had just been through—the Jew!" (T 130).

The peasants fail to see that Ramzin, rather than Kristianpoller, is the "devil" who through his deadly artifices has defiled the chapel. While their religious belief is naive, it runs deep and should suffice to tell them that by turning them into brutes, Ramzin debased, and led them to debase, the divine image in which they themselves were created.

Throughout the chapel episode and the immediately ensuing pogrom episode, Roth's narrator figures eloquently and movingly. As both objective external observer and compassionate commentator from within the circle of the endangered Jews, he illuminates the outburst of violence in Koropta. Probing the psyche of the assembled peasants and soldiers, he lays bare the currents of religious prejudice, ethnic hatred, and sexual aggression that underlie their religious fervor and turn them into a raging mob. Shame and self-restraint, the barriers erected by conscience in order to insure communal and individual well-being, succumb to the base forces of instinct. Almost at the same moment that the onlookers' shameless gawking, excited by Ramzin's drawings, yields to loving adoration of the revealed Holy Virgin, the peasants and soldiers erupt in blind hatred, first against the falsely accused Kristianpoller and then the community of his fellow Jews. In the end, Koropta presents a scene of pillage, destruction, and human misery.

Inasmuch as Tarabas has grossly neglected his duty to maintain order, he bears indirect guilt for the outbreak of the pogrom. But, despite a humiliating rebuke from his commanding general, he shows scant awareness of his dereliction. The first glimmer that his mighty self may be illusory and his existence false stems from a disarming exchange with Kristianpoller, the scared but clear-witted object of his rage over the day's events. His true awakening, however, results from a chance meeting with the sexton Shemariah, who has ventured out in the wake of the pogrom to rescue the fire-damaged Torah scrolls from the synagogue and, following Jewish custom, bury them in the cemetery. Although the narrator points to a direct connection between the fate of his protagonist and his abuse of the Jew Shemariah—in a scene redolent of Dostoyevsky, Tarabas sadistically rips out his beard—Tarabas's "dire aberration" (*T* 118) would, in fact, have been just as plausible without the pogrom so that, at best, the narrative link is indirect.

As Roth's letters to the Swiss theater critic Carl Seelig show, he himself was dissatisfied with the novel: "My book no longer pleases me a bit" (*BR* 319), he declared on 12 March 1934; on 7 July of the same year, he wrote emphatically: "It is *bad*" (*BR* 347). The reasons for this unhappiness remain a matter of speculation. Perhaps Roth recognized that his plot lacked unity, that for a long stretch, until Tarabas's abuse of the helpless Shemariah, the pogrom narrative wholly overshadows the story of his protagonist. Perhaps, too, Roth realized that he had failed convincingly to clarify Tarabas's awakening to remorse for his many trespasses in life, and thus also to clarify his repentance. In fact, Tarabas's progression from sin to atonement, from murderer to saint, conspicuously lacks the motivation that would make it psychologically credible.

Yet, there are hints enough in the novel that Tarabas's lifelong rebellion against the moral and civic order is rooted in the antagonistic relationship between the son and his authoritative father. The elder Tarabas orders his son from his home the first time because the younger Tarabas has joined a revolutionary society, that is, he has committed an act of rebellion. The second banishment occurs when the father discovers that, under his roof, Tarabas has slept with his young cousin Maria, a pseudo-adopted daughter of the family. This classical father-son conflict would seem all the more significant as Roth later mirrors it in the relationship between Tarabas's victim Shemariah and the latter's own renegade son. Indeed, Roth grants this particular substory marked attention (and even has the son somewhat dubiously cross Tarabas's path during the war). But he joins the two family stories all too superficially, more through happenstance than psychological plausibility. Although the father-son drama clearly occupied him, he missed the chance to thematize it in a way that would credibly motivate the critical turning point in his protagonist's life.

As a result of his violence against Shemariah, Tarabas believes that the prophesy of the gypsy woman in New York that he would become a murderer has fulfilled itself. This belief sets him on his path to atonement: "It seemed to him in that moment as though he had shouldered an infinitely heavy burden, but as though at the same time he had been delivered of another, unspeakably more oppressive still. His state was that of a man who, with a load at his feet which he has been condemned countless years ago to lift, knows that he has become laden with it at last, but without conscious action on his own part—as though it had put itself alive upon his back. He bent beneath its weight" (T 192–93).

When the local priest tells Tarabas that he can offer consolation but not absolution for his deed, the mighty division commander sheds his uniform and becomes a humble wanderer. The man who had been unable to put down roots now accepts his homelessness as an act of penance. Roaming the highways, he seeks "troubles and suffering and harsh treatment" (T 203). For food and shelter he is dependent on the compassion of the country folk; at times, he sleeps in abandoned huts and railway cars. Ragged and deathly sick, yet inwardly at peace, he returns to Koropta where, unrecognized, he begs a piece of bread from Shemariah—who, as a result of the pogrom, has become deranged. Tarabas's journey ends only when he has attained forgiveness from him for having trespassed against his humanity. Too weak to leave the nearby monastery where he lies dying, Tarabas asks the monk Eustachius to carry his message of contrition to Shemariah. In a moment of serene clarity, Shemariah, the most helpless of his victims, forgives him. With that the gypsy's prophesy fulfills itself that Tarabas would "sin and atone—and both upon this earth."

At the start of the last chapter, the narrator jumps forward in time from the history of Nicholas Tarabas by revealing that fifteen years have passed since his death. Meanwhile, the town of Koropta has been rebuilt "according to the western-European pattern" (T 270), that is, without regard for the past, and the young generation knows nothing of "the old story" (*T* 271). The sole keepers of it are Kristianpoller and the merchant Nissen Pichenik, who sometimes still talk of Tarabas and his strange fate. Although the resourceful Kristianpoller has restored the shed to be a chapel, thus drawing the peasants to his inn after Sunday mass, the new social order has brought a general profanation of daily life with it. The people seldom pray, and thus the special aura of the chapel has gradually dissipated. The White Eagle Inn still stands, however, and thrives in the new era of peaceful prosperity. When the visiting hop merchants inquire about the curious grave in the churchyard and ask whether the Jews still fear misfortune, Kristianpoller wisely explains that "people forget"; they forget the fears and the terrors, for they "want to live" (*T* 272–73). Amid silent Jewish memories and the social change of a new time, Kristianpoller and his inn remain and bear witness to generations-old tradition and historical continuity. In this way, their story transcends that of the once mighty Nicholas Tarabas, who had been but "a guest on earth."

## The Ballad of the Hundred Days

In 1934, during a time he described to Stefan Zweig as one of great personal distress (*BR* 339), Roth reworked a series of journalistic pieces into the apocalyptic book-essay *Der Antichrist* (1934; Antichrist). In another letter to Zweig, he declared that this new book was "a thousand times better than 'Tarabas'" (*BR* 320) and curiously called it a novel, although it actually constitutes an odd composite of religious vision, cultural criticism, and political polemics. The book derived its title from the early Christian notion of the Antichrist as the earthly denier of Jesus the Messiah.[3] With prophetic fervor, Roth condemns the Antichrist in his modern-day manifestations as National Socialism, Communism, anti-Semitism, and the corruptive civilization of technology. In the chapter "The Red Earth," his first-person narrator journeys to the Soviet Union and—as in Roth's earlier series "Travels in Russia," but now in the exalted tones of a seer—denounces the false social messianism he finds there. Consistent with his pronounced cultural conservatism, Roth also assails the signs of the Antichrist among western European Jewry, whose materialism and assimilationist ambitions he contrasts with the traditional religious and social values of the *Ostjuden*—this, too, a theme from an earlier series, *Juden auf Wanderschaft* (1927; *The Wandering Jews*); and, attacking the Vatican's 1933 Concordat with Nazi Germany, he also brands the Antichrist within the Catholic Church itself.

Conspicuously, Roth locates the gravest threat to modern civilization in the world film capital of Hollywood. In his metaphysical aesthetics, the medium of the film, in a fatefully ironic twist, turns the actors, or "originals," who have sold themselves to Hollywood, into the "alter egos" of their screen "shadows." Accordingly, moviegoers, as "shadow worshippers," become "not the *alter egos* of their own shadows, . . . but even less—namely, the *alter egos* of other people's shadows."[4] These latter "alter egos," immortalized in their separate screen existence, will outlive both the actor and alter ego. Having sold their lives, the originals have also sold their deaths and thus the possibility of personal salvation. For Roth, then, the cinema becomes "a Hades of the living" and Hollywood transmutes into a *Hölle-Wut,* or "raging hell."[5] In a letter to Zweig, written immediately after he had completed the manuscript, he condemned the cinema as "the prelude to the end of the world" (*BR* 339).

For all of its emotional excess—not only here but throughout *Antichrist*— Roth's diatribe against the evils of a materialistic epoch rests on a critical view of modernity that can claim intrinsic validity. With effort, that is, one can make good sense of it. Yet one need only contrast his apocalyptic visions with, for one, the film criticism of his fellow exile, the cultural theoretician Siegfried Kracauer (1889–1966), to recognize also the interpretive limitations of Roth's subjectivism.[6] Whereas Kracauer firmly grounds his analyses in the sociological, economic, and ideological currents of his time, *Antichrist* starkly evidences Roth's growing bent during his exile years to view historical events idiosyncratically, and to subordinate reason to belief and concrete analysis, which had never been his strength, to either passionate advocacy or condemnation. The consequences of these tendencies for his fictional work become glaringly clear in the Napoleon novel *Die hundert Tage* (1935; The Ballad of the Hundred Days), which followed *Tarabas.* As its title suggests, the novel depicts the hundred days between Napoleon's triumphant return to Paris from exile on St. Elba on 20 March 1815 and his second abdication and flight from France after the defeat on 18 June 1815 at Waterloo. In a letter of 17 November 1934 to his French translator Blanche Gidon, Roth outlined the theme of his new book. What attracted him to the figure of Napoleon, he explained, was his transformation from a god to a mortal: "Je voudrais faire un *'humble'* d'un 'grand.' C'est visiblement la *punition de Dieu,* la première fois dans l'histoire moderne. Napoleon abaissé: voilà le symbole d'une âme humaine absolument terrestre qui s'abaisse et qui s'èléve à même temps" (*BR* 395).

Written at a time when Roth's ambiguous Catholic leanings were growing ever more explicit (as *Tarabas* makes clear), *The Ballad of the Hundred Days* was to be anchored in a religious understanding of Napoleon's destiny. The emperor's descent from the heights of worldly grandeur to humility, according to Roth an event unique in modern history, would result as a punishment by God. Given this thematic design, the legendary tone for which Roth had gained renown in *Job* and *The Radetzky March* resounds almost of necessity throughout the novel; and since Roth's larger-than-life hero will eventually be humbled, oftentimes this tone is tinged with irony. That Roth additionally employs the Job motif at critical junctures of Napoleon's career underscores the legendary aspect of Napoleon's fate, but at the same time entails the risk of sentimentality or even pathos, something already inherent to Roth's narrative strategy. After Napoleon's defeat at Waterloo, for example, the retreating emperor hears a peasant pronounce to his neighbor in the silent throng outside his posting-station: "That is not the Emperor Napoleon! That is Job! That is not the emperor!"[7] To intensify the effect of his biblical analogy, Roth twice echoes these words, first from the inner self of his protagonist, then, as an affirmation of their truth, from that of his narrator:

> At once the Emperor turned. "Let us go! Forward!" he said to General Gouraud.
> He entered his coach. "That is Job! That is Job!" rang in his ears.
> "The Emperor Job!" the wheels repeated.
> The Emperor Job continued on his way to Paris (*HD* 213).

Despite such palpable lapses into melodrama, the practiced storyteller Roth manages to cast his spell. What seizes on the reader's imagination, however, and helps make the portrayal as affecting as it is, at least episodically, is the sheer drama of Napoleon's fate. The skill with which Roth orchestrates his dramatic effects is shown by the emperor's dream the night before he surrenders to the Royalists. Returning in the dream to the days of his greatest power, Napoleon explains to the pope why he has summoned him from Rome to France: "I have brought Heaven down to earth. It is not seemly that I should make a pilgrimage to Rome! What is Rome compared with Heaven? The stars are my friends! What is the Holy See compared with the stars? I want the imperial crown. I wish to be anointed. The stars themselves, the divine stars, have given me their blessing" (*HD* 273). In defiance of the divine representative, Napoleon sees himself as the Promethean figure he aspires to become in the eyes of the French people and, through his triumphs, actually does become. For, almost literally, the masses idolize him. Their historical destiny is bound to his, and Napoleon's eventual descent from the heights of power finds a narrative parallel in their collective tragedy. In turn, this drama is symbolically represented in the figure of the lowly young Corsican court servant Angela Petri, whose adoring loyalty to her emperor and its vicissitudes form the entire content of Book Two of the novel's four books, while the last of the four is devoted to her violent end at the hands of the Royalists.

Napoleon's transformation from a "grand" into a "humble" follows an uneven path. For a long while, the emperor vacillates between the temptations of earthly might and submission to the will of God. Even when he is able to admit to himself that he no longer loves power but rather lowliness, that he wishes to be "humble and happy," to hold a cross rather than a crown (*HD* 230), his accustomed pride remains. This inner conflict of the sovereign ready to renounce his scepter crystallizes on the night following Napoleon's abdication. As he had done earlier in both *Job* and *The Radetzky March,* Roth evokes the motif of the lonely creature beneath the vast arch of the star-illumined heavens and reflects in it the polarities in his hero's soul:

> That night he again felt he could pierce the falsely sublime intentions of the Ruler of the Universe. He had never acknowledged the existence of God, but now he believed he could understand His ways. He, the Emperor, believed that God was an Emperor like himself, but wiser, more prudent, and therefore more enduring. He, the Emperor Napoleon, had been foolish out of magnanimity. It was magnanimity that had lost him his power. If it had not been for his magnanimity, he too might have been God, might have created the blue arch of the heavens, might have regulated the brilliance and the orbits of the stars, directed the destiny of mankind and the course of the winds, the passage of the clouds and the flight of the birds. But he, the Emperor Napoleon, was more modest than God, careless and generous, unthinking and magnanimous. (*HD* 231)

Here Napoleon is still the *incroyant* that, in the truest sense, he remains until the end of the novel. He perceives God as the creator of the universe, the sovereign of the world, but with false intentions and, except for his "magnanimity," Napoleon believes he himself could have replaced God on the divine throne. To his brother Jerome, Napoleon confesses that he does not yet believe in God, but that he has begun to have a premonition of God's power (*HD* 236). At this point, however, the transformation that Roth described in his letter to Blanche Gidon as the prime concern of his novel has already taken place. Napoleon has willingly renounced his throne and gone from being a "grand" to a "humble." To be sure, his confession to Jerome alludes to an element of religious belief in this process, but this belief is still a nascent one. Its depth and the role it may have played in Napoleon's actions elude determination. Neither the emperor's own words nor the narrator's stance justify the notion that in the end Napoleon has returned to the bosom of religion or the church. Even after he has uttered his wish for a cross, he declares that he does not yet believe in God.

A clear discrepancy separates Roth's original plan for *The Ballad of the Hundred Days* and its realization. For this reason, one can only accept the author's understanding of it reservedly. The wholly personal tale of Napoleon's transformation from a demi-god to a God-seeker strains to define itself within the novel's broad historical setting, the more so as Roth endows his protagonist with features that place him alongside still other grand and destructive leaders in modern history. He portrays a Napoleon driven to secure the devotion of the masses and bring them under his seductive sway, an iron-willed leader captured by dreams of power and conquest. Seen within the historical context of the Third Reich, the analogy with Hitler clearly suggests itself. Yet, the novel's religious themes of humility and repentance just as clearly separate Roth's literary figure from the Nazi dictator and his contemporary counterparts.

Once earlier, in the case of *The Radetzky March,* Roth subsequently lamented his recourse to history as a narrative subject. Yet, in that work he had successfully portrayed a momentous historical epoch through the generational story of a single family, the Trottas. In *The Ballad of the Hundred Days,* by contrast, history became the mere backdrop to the private tale of Napoleon's conversion. Aware that he had put himself at odds with his own intentions, Roth all too conspicuously resorted to an exaggerated lyricism in order to lend epic breadth to the private turns of his hero's fate. Inasmuch as he, too, was unhappy with the outcome of the novel, he concurred with its general reception by the critics. But aside from his renewed regret at having drawn on historical material, his self-criticism reflects the same penchant that contributed to the novel's failings. In an undated letter to his fellow writer-in-exile René Schickele, possibly penned while he was still writing the book, Roth denounced his undertaking as reprehensible ("Es ist was Gottloses drin") and declared that the Antichrist himself had lured him to it (*BR* 412).

## Confession of a Murderer

Besides the torment over the fate of his wife in Austria, Roth's distress in exile was deepened by yet another unhappy turn in his personal affairs. By 1936 his relationship with Andrea Manga Bell, the half-German, half-Cuban separated wife of a Cameroon prince, whom he had met in Berlin in 1929, had reached the breaking point. The two had lived together from 1931 on, and since her two children received no support from their father in Africa, Roth had felt himself bound to provide for them too. This and still other tribulations pushed him to both his physical and artistic limits. After *Beichte eines Mörders, erzählt in einer Nacht* (Confession of a Murderer: Told in One Night) appeared in 1936, he confided in a letter of 4 May 1936 to Stefan Zweig that the new novel was "very weak," that he had written it too quickly (*BR* 469). While Zweig praised the work for its symmetry and the artistic wholeness of its Russian ambiance, he remarked that in recent years Roth had stretched the plots of his stories beyond their natural proportions (*BR* 478).

Common to the four novels Roth published between 1934 and 1937 are the religious themes of evil and goodness, hubris and fall, sin and repentance. With the exception of *The Ballad of the Hundred Days,* in each of the others— *Tarabas, Confession of a Murderer,* and *Weights and Measures*—Roth returned to the Slavic borderlands of his boyhood for his settings and many of his figures. Thematically, and by virtue of shared major motifs, *Confession of a Murderer* stands closest of all to *Tarabas.* Significant parts of both works are set in Russia; in both the protagonist is weighted down by the belief that he has committed a murder—in Semyon Golubchik's case a double murder—and in each instance it turns out that the presumed victim has survived the violent attack. Like Tarabas, Semyon Golubchik, the main figure of *Confession of a Murderer,* is rescued from police pursuit by the outbreak of the First World War. Furthermore, at the center of both novels stands the moral depravity of the protagonist; and in each he awakens to the realization of his criminal nature after he has brutally mistreated or betrayed an innocent person. That both victims are *Ostjuden*—in *Tarabas* the sexton Shemariah, in *Confession of a Murderer* the social revolutionary Channa Lea Rifkin—is surely more than coincidence. More likely, Roth's conviction that Europe's Jews were faced with disaster led him to express compassion with his east European kin by portraying them as the defenseless victims of violence at the hands of evil perpetrators.[8] It is likewise possible—perhaps even probable—that in this way Roth also wished to assuage feelings of personal guilt at having abandoned his fellow Jews when he left Brody with the intent to assimilate in the west.

The "confession" of the book's title, the tale, that is, of the Russian secret agent Golubchik, stationed as an informer in Paris, is framed by the story of an unnamed writer, likewise narrated in the first person. Adding a further note of intrigue to the suspenseful novel is that this framework narrator bears the earmarks of Roth himself. Like Roth, he fought in the First World War, speaks Russian, and, commissioned by a leading newspaper, traveled as a journalist in the Soviet Union. He, too, lives in a hotel on the left bank of the Seine, tends to overindulge in alcohol, and enjoys Russian cooking and Russian social ways in general. This personal disposition leads him to frequent the restaurant Tari-Bari opposite his hotel, where one night, as a silent listener in a circle of Russian émigrés, he hears Golubchik recite his odd story.

"Our murderer," as the regular patrons describe the protagonist with indulgent humor, begins his confession at midnight, after the closing hour, and ends it as the first light of morning creeps though the closed shutters. With time compressions, it embraces his entire life, from his boyhood almost to the hour of narration, and ends, unexpectedly, with a grotesque real-life epilogue that places his fate in an even stranger light than his confession already had.

Unsparingly, Golubchik relates his descent into degradation, a process that begins with the inability of the young man to live with his family name. As the illegitimate son of wealthy Prince Krapotkin, he thirsts to acquire the lofty name of his natural father and to cast off the name of his adoptive father, the forester Golubchik. To clarify the protagonist's compulsively aired aversion to his surname, a note explains, although inadequately, that in Russian "golubchik" means "little dove."[9] Alongside this literal meaning, however, the noun "golubchik" contains a second, figurative meaning. In everyday Russian usage, as a term of endearment it is akin to "darling" or "sweetheart," and it is this syrupy appellation that its bearer rejects as particularly shameful.[10]

Golubchik's quest to gain what he considers his birthright is blocked by a second illegitimate offspring of the prince, Sergei Krapotkin, who is actually the natural son of Princess Krapotkin and a Frenchman, and is thus not bound to the prince through ties of blood. However, the prince recognizes Sergei as his son, whereas he utterly spurns Golubchik. As a result, Golubchik makes it his life's mission to destroy his favored "stepbrother." But even though he enters the service of the powerful and feared Ochrana, the Russian secret police, each of his attempts to kill his rival is thwarted by the greater power of the name Krapotkin.

More and more, the spy Golubchik becomes enmeshed in treachery and guilt. His guide along this shameful path is a mysterious Hungarian, Jenö Lakatos, whom the still quite young Golubchik first met in Odessa, where he had gone to demand his filial rights from the prince. Repeatedly, Lakatos will cross Golubchik's path in eerie and destructive ways, so that Golubchik soon sees in him the devil incarnate and the source of his bottomless plunge into evil. Just as he himself believes absolutely in the hellish provenance of the elegantly limping Hungarian, in the end the framework narrator also grows to fear him. When a suave, black-haired, limping stranger, whose yellow baggage bears the "blood-red" initials J. L., checks into his hotel and is assigned the adjoining room, the narrator speedily forsakes his quarters there.

The names Golubchik and Krapotkin are more than mere names. Taken together, they describe a deep-seated personal conflict that Roth's protagonist is too weak to resolve. The false life he leads in Paris under the name of Krapotkin—upon his wish, the Moscow secret police issued him a passport with this name—prevents him from achieving an authentic existence of his own. He himself realizes that by casting off the name Golubchik by means of a lie, he has betrayed himself and fallen still deeper into guilt. Yet, the name Krapotkin is infused with such power that a return to morality appears impossible: "I was already in the depths of Hell. Yes, I was already a hardened servitor of Hell, and still—I felt it at that moment—the one, stupid, blind, driving-force of my life was my chagrin at the name of Golubchik and at the degradation to which I considered I had been subjected, and my mania to become a Krapotkin at any price. I still believed that through cunning and treachery I could wipe out what I deemed to be the stigma in my life. But I only heaped disgrace after disgrace upon my own miserable head" (*CM* 136).

In Paris, the covetous and deceitful fashion model Lutetia leads Golubchik further on his ignominious path. The two had first met in Saint Petersburg and she has now entangled him in a love-hate relationship. In a short time, Golubchik finds himself hard pressed to provide her with the comforts and luxuries she desires, but fulfills her wishes nonetheless. Kept by him, she exchanges her room in a tawdry hotel for a *maisonette* near the Champs Elysées, "one of those houses," Golubchik explains, "which at that time used to be called 'love-nests'" (*CM* 151). Ironically, Lutetia has her new quarters papered with the same parrot pattern that earlier had covered the walls of her hotel room and so repelled her lover—"parrots," Golubchik declares bitterly, "that had all the qualities of doves" (*CM* 145). Thus, in Lutetia's presence he is constantly reminded of his true identity, of the "little dove" he is fated to remain despite his legitimation by the secret police as a Krapotkin. Prey to the kindred vices of suspicion and jealousy, when he discovers Lutetia in the embrace of his hated stepbrother, Sergei Krapotkin, he attacks them murderously and leaves them for dead.

Sought by the police, Golubchik returns to Russia, enlists in the army and, plagued by his conscience, yearns to gain atonement by dying in battle. But death shuns him. When the war ends, he returns to Paris and finds Lutetia, who has survived her injuries; and in the Jardin du Luxembourg, he encounters by chance his rival, the supposedly murdered Sergei Krapotkin, whose injuries have left him lame and feeble-minded. To Sergei's query he answers tersely that yes, Lutetia is still alive, and with this detail the supposed murderer's midnight confession ends. Or almost. For, Golubchik's story is unpredictably extended beyond its formal conclusion when, in the early morning hour, Lutetia turns up at the Tari-Bari screeching frightfully—in search of her husband, Golubchik. The framework narrator recounts: "She looked more like an overgrown, emaciated bird than a woman" (*CM* 217). Before she retreats—Golubchik had quickly hidden under a table—she casts "a few vicious and inhumanly sharp [bird] glances round the room."[11] For the reader, it thus becomes evident why Golubchik can be found so often at the Tari-Bari: he, the little dove, finds life with this repellent, overgrown bird intolerable, and he regularly flees his domestic "love-nest" for the comforting atmosphere of the Russian restaurant.

Golubchik's description of his postwar reunion with Lutetia as "unbelievably banal, ridiculous, even grotesque" (*CM* 215) describes perfectly the episode that follows his confession. To that point, the assurance to the reader by Roth's framework narrator that—contrary to what the "murderer" himself insists—Golubchik's tale will be neither "short nor commonplace" (*CM* 18) can go uncontested. Golubchik's confession has, indeed, proved engrossing in all respects. But when the unexpected postlude sends its obviously henpecked narrator scurrying under the table, the confession itself forfeits its poignancy as a story of obsessive ambition and fall. Instead, it disintegrates into the "tragedy of banality" that Golubchik himself saw in his reunion with Lutetia (*CM* 215).

When Golubchik does feel genuine remorse and unsparingly indicts himself as a scoundrel, it is for his deception first of the young and wholly innocent Russian-Jewish anarchist Komrower, and then of the likewise Russian-Jewish social revolutionary Channa Lea Rifkin and her crippled brother. In both instances he commits an act of base betrayal in order to finance Lutetia's desires with the reward money he receives from the Ochrana. Deplorable as the fate of the disabled Sergei Krapotkin may be, the real tragedy of the novel revolves around the Rifkins, who, as Golubchik remarks to his listeners, "were probably the only ones [he] had killed" (*CM* 215). To the detriment of the novel, however, neither Rifkin is developed as a character, and inasmuch as Golubchik's guilt does not lead to any act of penitence by him, their story remains episodic. In the end, then, Golubchik's confession better serves the outward aims of a psychological suspense novel than that of a true catharsis on the part of its narrator (although this is what the book's title and the assurances of Roth's framework narrator lead one to expect). Indeed, the title itself turns out to be one of the novel's most salient ironies, since, in contrast to his uncertain listeners, Golubchik knows at the time of his narration that he has murdered neither the young Krapotkin nor Lutetia; and at no point does he confess to even the slightest contrition at his fervently nurtured plan to kill his rival or at his violent, if failed, attack on both him and his mistress. Rather, he wards off any pangs of moral or criminal guilt by persuading himself that, as a lowly Golubchik, he had been afflicted with an outrageous fate and that this entirely justifies his vengeful deeds. In addition to the greater appeal to readers, Roth most likely had such an ironic effect in mind when he scrapped his rather bland working title for the novel, "Der Stammgast" (The Regular Patron), for the more suggestive *Confession of a Murderer.*

## Weights and Measures

In its entirety, Roth's next novel, *Das falsche Gewicht: Die Geschichte eines Eichmeisters* (1937; Weights and Measures), is set in the fictitiously named district of Zlotogrod "in the remote eastern part of the monarchy."[12] It takes place,

70

that is, in the author's native Galicia, and for the most part in the village of Szwaby, which conspicuously bears the same name as the Brody neighborhood in which Roth was born. Although Roth curiously insisted at one point that his setting was Bukovina, he clearly had Galicia before his inner eye as he wrote the novel. As though to complete his journey home, he populated the story with a flock of secondary figures familiar to the reader from earlier works, all of them Slavs or east European Jews. From *Job* he summoned Mendel Singer, again as a poor and pious children's teacher, the Russian peasant Sameshkin, now a chestnut roaster, and the smuggler Kapturak, who in *The Radetzky March* ran the gambling casino in the younger Trotta's Galician garrison town. From *The Radetzky March* he called forth the constabulary sergeant Slama and Trotta's Ruthenian orderly Onufrij. And from *Tarabas* Roth revived the shopkeeper Nissen Pichenik, who now reappeared as a corals dealer. But far from representing a wishful flight from the insecurities of exile to the familiar environs of a less precarious time, *Weights and Measures* is pervaded by an atmosphere of bleakness and death. It depicts the decline of its protagonist from an ordered life to moral and physical dissolution and, in the end, a violent demise.

The linear plot of the novel can be summarized as follows: After twelve years of service in an artillery regiment, the noncommissioned officer Anselm Eibenschütz, prodded by his wife, quits military service. As a government weights and measures inspector, he is assigned to the remote and inhospitable backwaters of Zlotogrod, where the population consists mainly of small Jewish shopkeepers and traders who struggle to eke out their sustenance. (In passing, the narrator remarks that Eibenschütz himself was "of Jewish stock" and has him briefly recall his orthodox grandfather's funeral [*WM* 59]. However, this circumstance remains entirely without consequence for the protagonist's person or the course of the story.) Because of his unbending honesty and strict insistence on the letter of the law, Eibenschütz incurs fear and hostility among the town dwellers. Soon, his loneliness and the loveless marriage to his wife of five years prove intolerable. After his wife betrays him with his young office scribe, Nowak, with whom she bears a child, Eibenschütz becomes captive to his passion for the gypsy Euphemia Nikitsch, the lover of the Szwaby tavern owner, smuggler, and reputed murderer, Jadlowker. Eibenschütz cleverly removes his rival by charging him with a crime, for which Jadlowker is sentenced to prison for two years, and then proceeds to take up quarters in the tavern with Nikitsch. However, his dubious luck is disrupted when her former lover, the chestnut roaster Sameshkin from Slovenia, turns up at the tavern. Debased by raw passion and drink, Eibenschütz sees himself stymied and isolated on all sides. After a cholera epidemic claims his wife and her child, he begins to long for death. He drinks heavily and neglects his appearance. Finally, in an act of revenge, he is killed by the always dangerous Jadlowker, who has escaped from prison.

This straightforward plot finds its counterpart in Roth's equally uncompli-cated depiction of the novel's characters, who emerge as exemplars of single fixed qualities that define their individual existences. The main figure, Eiben-schütz, embodies a sense of justice so rigid as to blind him to the simple, humane insight that in everyday practice the law must be tempered by compassion. Sim-ilarly, Eibenschütz's antagonist, tavern keeper Jadlowker, appears as lawlessness and violence incarnate, while the gypsy Nikitsch figures in her pure sensuality as the temptress through and through. Still others of the book's more or less prominent players can be typified in like manner.[13] But while they lack the com-plexity of character that would make them deeply engaging literary creations, through the sheer concreteness of their portrayal they work the kind of raw emo-tive effect on the reader as does an expressionist woodcut by, say, Erich Heckel, Emil Nolde, Karl Schmidt-Rotluff, or Käthe Kollwitz.[14]

In *Weights and Measures,* as in the three novels that preceded it, Roth focused entirely on an individual's fate. At the same time, however, he attempted to join his central theme of the protagonist's self-alienation and moral decline with the religious theme of sin and repentance which occupied him intensely at this time. In his dying moments, Eibenschütz hallucinates that the Great Weights Inspector has come to inspect *his* "weights," to pass judgment, that is, on the rightness or wrongness of his dealings with others. With wonderment, Eiben-schütz hears from him the paradoxical verdict: "All your weights are false, and yet they are all correct. So we shall not report you! We believe that all of your weights are correct" (*WM* 149). Thus, it would appear that Eibenschütz dies as the recipient of God's grace—despite the fact that he had invariably stifled the compassion that sometimes stirred in him, and, through his blind correctness, harmed the already afflicted town dwellers whose livelihoods were subject to his authority.

In the early novel *Rebellion,* Andreas Pum renounces God's grace as his indi-vidual protest against the injustices of the social order. Eibenschütz, on the other hand, has forfeited all right to accept such grace. To be sure, the weights of the poor traders of Zlotogrod are false, but theirs is a daily struggle for existence, without prospect of an easier lot. Under such circumstances, the standards for fair dealings became subject to another, less exacting type of social contract, tolerated as a necessity by both parties to even the smallest transaction. Even though Eiben-schütz was not driven to his harsh treatment of the fearful townspeople by evil intent but rather by a trait of character into which he himself had no insight, Roth's moral equation at the end still dissolves into quasi-metaphysical sentimentality. Possibly, however, a kinder consideration can be offered to help resolve the story's problematic conclusion. In his memoirs, the Russian writer Ilya Ehrenburg recalls a conversation with Roth about the novel in which Roth told him that the Great Weights Inspector himself denied the existence of "exact scales."[15] Perhaps this assurance describes the measure by which Roth wishcd to judge the "sinners" who stand at the center of his later novels and stories—men like Nicholas Tarabas, Semyon Golubchik, and Anselm Eibenschütz. As uncertain and insecure human beings, buffeted by fickle fortune, he might appeal, they, like all of us, are apt to err and stumble, and thus they merit our understanding. That Roth, long plagued by guilt over the fate of his wife, was also appealing with this argument for a benevolent judgment of his own person, seems likely enough. In his conversation with Ehrenburg, he identified expressly with his ill-fated protagonist Eibenschütz. "My inspector," he declared, "lives badly and confused: Like me."[16]

# CHAPTER 6

# The Exile Years, 1938–1939

## Return to the Theme of Austria

### *The Tale of the 1002nd Night*

*Die Geschichte von der 1002. Nacht* (The Tale of the 1002nd Night) appeared in Holland in the spring of 1939, only weeks before Roth's death. For Roth as well as his Dutch publisher, the story of its production was trying. On the publisher's side, it was rife with pleas that Roth submit the corrected manuscript, with hopes disappointed, and with mounting irritation. On Roth's side, there were repeated failures to meet deadlines, explanations and promises, prideful demands for fees, and urgent appeals for them. Before Roth finally presented a reworked version of the manuscript, he had already consumed his advance payments for it. To make matters worse, he had received further payment for a second novel, *The Emperor's Tomb,* which he had promised to complete by the fall of 1937. When the time came, however, he had written barely more than a dozen pages and had still to meet his obligations for *The Tale of the 1002nd Night.*[1]

Altogether, these circumstances typify Roth's material and psychological plight as a writer in exile. Five years after he fled Germany, the Nazi Anschluss of Austria deprived him of his last sources of income there—both his journalistic work and the possibilities of selling film rights. Meanwhile, the burden of care for his mentally ill wife, who was confined first in one Austrian clinic, then another, continued to strain his severely limited means. For support he had become increasingly dependent on publisher advances and loans from his friends in exile, above all the faithful and forbearing Stefan Zweig. By this time, too, his steady drinking had taken a heavy toll; his liver was diseased, and in 1938 he suffered a heart attack. Yet, the exigencies of debts and deadlines compelled him to increase his already hectic journalistic and literary output. As a result, he wrote quickly, and his books appeared in such rapid succession that he felt he had ruined his reputation.

Under such unabating stress, it is little wonder that Roth's writing became susceptible to stylistic weaknesses, and that these brought criticism from his reviewers. Particularly *The Ballad of the Hundred Days* and *Weights and Measures* exhibit the misuse of narrative devices that in better times Roth had employed more discriminately and felicitously. Too often now he took recourse for effect to dramatic, even mystical twists of plot, and to the mannered repetition of a stock repertoire of images, turns of phrase, and syntactical patterns familiar to his readers from earlier works. Yet, amid the travails of his last years, the doomed author, as though touched by grace, wrote the novel that can stand alongside *The Radetzky March* as his most accomplished work. In *The Tale of the 1002nd Night,* the qualities that distinguish Roth's finest writing emerged once more in brilliant array: the musicality of his language, the precision and vividness of his descriptions of persons and locales, the evocation of mood and atmosphere in their subtlest shadings, and the legendary tone for which he had won fame in *Job* and now once more masterfully controlled. With his nostalgia for the past held in check by an unblinking realism, in *The Tale of the 1002nd Night* Roth again recalled the sunken world of the Habsburg Monarchy that he had first celebrated in *The Radetzky March.*

With its frame structure and flashback episodes, the novel is intricately fashioned and its precise chronology is elusive. That Roth aimed for just this effect becomes apparent in his very first sentence: "In the spring of the year 18__, the Shah-in-Shah, the great, exalted, and holy monarch, the absolute ruler and overlord of all the lands of Persia, began to feel a sense of malaise of a kind he had never before experienced."[2] Advised by his chief eunuch to seek "variety," something both know to be illusory, the shah sets sail for a visit to the royal court in Vienna. While in all likelihood this episode was inspired by an actual visit of the shah to Vienna in 1873, Roth obliquely dates his beginning by placing it two hundred years after "the most terrifying of all Muslims had laid siege to Vienna" (*TN* 23), that is, after the failed Ottoman onslaught of 1683. More important than fidelity to history, however, the incomplete date of 18__ connects intriguingly with the novel's *Arabian Nights* title to conjure up notions of a fabled past abounding in exotic surprises. Yet almost from its start the narrative hints that Roth's contemporary retelling of an oriental tale will be refracted through the prism of ironic—at times bitterly ironic—humor. Indeed, throughout the novel, the fairy-tale magic that extends from the frame story into the main plot will be undercut again and again as life's harsh realities turn the lives of the principal figures into an anti-fairy tale. The story of the shah's visit to Vienna, which constitutes the actual *Arabian Nights* tale promised by the book's title, is particularly pervaded by multiple ironies of expectation and outcome.

Thanks to a farcical scheme contrived by the cavalry officer Baron Taittinger to ward off a scandal at the court, the shah spends the night in a Vienna brothel with Taittinger's erstwhile lover, meanwhile turned prostitute, Mizzi Schinagl. Thirsting for new experience, the shah, who at home commands a harem of 365 wives, fails to see through the hastily arranged disguise of the brothel's ordinary decor. Likewise, he succumbs to the illusion that he has gained the favors of the married Countess W., whom he espied at the emperor's ball and in whose arms he desires to explore the "erotic arts of the West" (*TN* 65). Although he learns of the ruse only years later, his nocturnal tryst with Countess W.'s look-alike affords him only momentary delight; quickly he is forced to acknowledge that life brings only stifling repetition. More than the insight that "desire and curiosity were an illusion," it was the shah's naive notions of the "exotic" West that turned his Viennese escapade into the "biggest disappointment of his life" (*TN* 66). Yet his visit would prove still more fateful for the three others entangled in it: Schinagl, rewarded by the shah with a precious necklace of pearls, the brothel owner Josephine Matzner, to whom the affair brings short-lived local celebrity, and the self-satisfied Taittinger, who soon spirals downward into depression and drink.

With a critical eye and at the same time the benevolence that one lost soul feels for another, Roth placed the cavalry officer Baron Alois Franz von Taittinger at the center of his novel; and he endowed him with qualities that make him brother to Arthur Schnitzler's fin-de-siècle Viennese playboy Anatol and second cousin, but kin nonetheless, to Hugo von Hofmannsthal's deeper, more refined and ethically responsible Count Kari Bühl, the main figure of the comedy *Der Schwierige*.[3] Roth endowed Taittinger with qualities, that is, that the playwright Hofmannsthal, in his schematic characterization "Preuße und Österreicher" (Prussian and Austrian) posited as typically Austrian.[4] With Bühl, the "difficult" man of Hofmannsthal's title, these qualitites find elevated, positive expression whereas with Taittinger they are manifested negatively throughout. While Taittinger lacks all talent for abstraction and dialectical thinking, he is possessed of a certain frivolous know-how that only brings him trouble. Self-absorbed to a fault, his lassitude and hedonism lead him from one personal crisis to another, the solutions to which he eagerly places in the hands of others. To matters that could become unpleasant for him he studiously shuts his eyes. And well-intentioned though he may be, he values his peace of mind above all else and does his best to keep the hapless Schinagl and their wayward illegitimate son at a safe distance. Perhaps because Taittinger seems so utterly helpless to take his worsening fate into his own hands, the reader finds it hard to deny him a measure of sympathy.

When in *The Radetzky March* Emperor Franz Joseph, recognizing his realm is in decline, whispers resignedly, "Da kann man nix machen!"—"What can you do?"—Roth's narrator adds by way of explanation: "For he was an Austrian" (*RM* 225). As the confession, witting or not, of an unperturbed fatalism, the phrase has attained popular status as an expression of the Austrian psyche. Spoken by the emperor, it is dignified by his acceptance of historical inevitability.

Just as aptly, Roth could have placed the same words in the mouth of Taittinger; indeed, as a byword for Taittinger's passivity in the face of self-created troubles he could have applied it as a motto to his book.

Distinctively Austrian, too, is the novel's ambiance. From the imperial city of Vienna and Taittinger's dreary Silesian garrison town to his decrepit estate deep in the Carpathians, Roth recaptures both the brilliance and the decay of Habsburg Austria in the last decades of the nineteenth century. In Vienna, Roth evokes a multitude of public and private places that until today uphold the city's fame: the coffee houses and stately hotels, the public parks with their military band concerts and other popular amusements, and, in their center, the imperial palace. From the outlying Sievering district of small shopkeepers, where Taittinger begins his ill-starred dalliance with Schinagl, to the Inner City with its palette of grand sights and lilting sounds, Roth resurrected the rich atmosphere of Golden Vienna, along with its dark and decadent underside. Additionally, to deepen the novel's local color and represent the multiethnic character of the monarchy, he drew on a broad cast of secondary figures from the most varied walks of life and social strata, with an equally diverse range of typifying surnames, including German, Italian, Hungarian, Slavic, and Jewish.

The plot of the novel after the shah's departure from Vienna chronicles the fateful consequences of the event in the lives of Taittinger, Schinagl, and Matzner. For the shah, the conflict between reality and illusion, which lies at the core of the frame episode, is resolved to the extent that he comes to realize that deception and error are inseparable from human existence, and like all mortals he, too, is subject to them. For Taittinger, Schinagl, and Matzner, the story of the shah's visit takes on a life of its own. Unable to overcome its effects, they are engulfed by them.

The outwardly appealing but selfish and shallow Taittinger learns in the end that it was only thanks to his self-willed ignorance that he had once been able to view the world so unproblematically; the categories he had devised to regulate his personal relations—people were either "charming," "so-so," or "tedious"—had betrayed him. Too late he recognizes that there are still other types, above all the "unknowable" ones. The aftermath of the story that he had once set in motion teaches him that life's episodes live on; "treacherous and invisible," following their own laws, they return with vengeful power (*TN* 235).

As another result of the shah's visit, Schinagl attains wealth when she pawns the shah's lavish gift of pearls. Her newly gained fortune leads her from the protective surroundings of the Matzner brothel into a wider world of luxury, whose hazards and allurements exceed her limited grasp of life. When she falls into the clutches of the scheming suitor Lissauer, anxieties and self-alienation overcome her. She longs for the safe haven that the brothel had provided her, but the knowledge that she has lost her way in life blocks a return to her former certainties. The pearls, which had seemingly brought her good fortune, become her undoing. Tricked into fraudulent dealings by her paramour, who promises to multiply her wealth, she lands in the Women's Penitentiary.

Just as surely, Matzner also falls victim to the repercussions of the story. After the duped Schinagl has bankrupted their commonly owned dry goods store, Matzner, irrationally fearing ruin, presses a lawsuit against her. For a short time Matzner basks in the notoriety of the case, but she soon finds herself forgotten and faced with old age and sickness. As it had Schinagl, the story robs her, too, of a once secure identity. The brothel falls on hard times, and she trades its familiar setting for an apartment in Vienna's genteel First District. Amid her new and unaccustomed environs, however, she must confront a scared self she had never before known because, fortuitously, the circumstances of her former life had shielded her from it. Her thoughts now revolve obsessively around the money she fears she must leave behind. Afflicted by her anxieties and avarice, she dies a freakish old woman.

It is, however, Taittinger whose fate Roth pursues most persistently and revealingly. Like Schinagl and, less directly, Matzner, he, too, is undone by the story. With his foolish collaboration, the small-time local reporter Lazik turns it into a scandalous series of dime booklets. The once privileged cavalry captain is then forced by disgrace to quit the military and, brought to grief by the frivolous neglect of his financial affairs, seek to restore his solvency on his estate "in the Ceterymentar district, buried deep in the snowy Carpathian mountains" (*TN* 87). But years of neglect have irreparably ruined the estate. Taittinger's disquietude and, above all, the fear of his alien surroundings parallel psychologically the condition of homelessness that marks the fate of his fellow conspirators in the story, Schinagl and Matzner. Despondently, he spends his evenings at the village tavern, where, bolstered by drink, he resolves to return to Vienna.

Discharged from the army, Taittinger is unhappily reunited with Schinagl and their repugnant adolescent son, Xandl. While he vaguely feels himself responsible for Schinagl's welfare, he passes his days without purpose. To compound his straits, he is threatened by Schinagl's new riffraff friends, Magdalene Kreutzer and Ignaz Trummer, into buying Schinagl a waxworks in the Prater amusement park. When Xandl comically bungles a holdup there and the papers reveal his parentage, Taittinger is barred by the War Ministry from rejoining the army. Shorn of the illusions that had once sustained him and unable to master the complexities of civilian life, the prematurely aged and forlorn baron shoots himself in his Vienna hotel room. When asked by a mutual acquaintance why he thought Taittinger killed himself, Lieutenant Colonel Kalergi answers simply: "I think he lost his way in life. It happens. A man can lose his way" (*TN* 251).

Less penetratingly than in the person of Carl Joseph von Trotta in *The Radetzky March,* but just as poignantly, Roth mirrored in Alois Franz von Taittinger the loss of inner direction, will, and vitality of intellect and spirit, which on the historical plane hastened Austria's downfall. At the time of the novel's setting, the troubles that were to overtake the monarchy in the next century were heard in Vienna only as faint rumblings on a distant horizon. Amid the thoughtless passions and empty pursuits that occupy Roth's figures and, seemingly, all of Vienna, they are not heard at all. "Far and wide," Roth's narrator comments, "the world was deeply, horribly at peace" (*TN* 138). Yet the darkness of Roth's own time, which had already descended as night over central Europe, hovers above the narrative. There can be little doubt that when Roth warns at its beginning of the new "Age of Prussia, the age of the Janissaries of Luther and Bismarck" (*TN* 23), he has Hitler in mind. Writing in a Prague journal in 1934, for example, he provocatively called Hitler a successor to Martin Luther;[5] and in 1939, he polemicized in an Austrian exile paper: "We could easily demonstrate from Germany's history since Luther that there was an entirely organic, natural, even *self-evident* progression from Luther by way of Frederick the Second, Bismarck, and [Emperor] Wilhelm to Hitler" (*W* 4:444–45).

The last two chapters of the novel add an epilogue, both lighthearted and bitter, to the beginning story of the shah's visit. Some fifteen years after his assignation in Frau Matzner's brothel (and ten days after Taittinger's burial), the shah returns to Vienna. He has grown older and wiser, and the addition to his harem of a fourteen-year-old delight from India brings him daily contentment. To assure him an unblemished stay, Schinagl's waxworks in the Prater, newly named "The World Bioscope Theater," has been closed for business until his departure. And with good reason: Seizing the propitious moment, Schinagl and her thuggish associates, Kreutzer and Trummer, had staged a tableau reenactment of the shah's earlier visit to Vienna. At its center Schinagl herself appears on a red throne, decked out in false pearls and diamonds, as "[t]he Viennese concubine, a child of the people from Sievering, conducted to the Shah by important public figures and subsequently ruler of the Harem in Persia" (*TN* 249). With this, Roth caps the theme of fateful illusions that runs through the novel. As though in a sideshow house of mirrors, with one reflected image more grotesque than the other, Schinagl appears as her own double, who herself had been a double: the "lie-in," that is, for the unobtainable Countess W. At that time she was the foolish yet innocent accomplice to Taittinger's deception; now, billed as "the shah's favorite wife," she knowingly perverts herself for a paying public

(*TN* 243). Among Roth's numerous heroines, most of whom are thoroughly dislikeable—the likeable ones tend to die early or otherwise soon fade from the scene—Schinagl is the most amply and sympathetically drawn; in the end, however, she sinks into garish opportunism.

The final words of Roth's anti-fairy tale may be heard as the author's personal verdict on the Austrian and German, and perhaps the entire western European, society of his own time. The artisan Tino Percoli, who creates the wax figures for Schinagl's "The World Bioscope Theater" and is privy to the old but still malignant story of the shah, laments: "I might be capable of making figures that have heart, conscience, passion, emotion, and decency. But there's no call for that at all in the world. People are only interested in monsters and freaks, so I give them their monsters. Monsters are what they want!" (*TN* 261). Through his fictional spokesman, Roth thus condemned the moral languor, human callousness, and self-deception that lay below the surface of the Gay Vienna of his tale and were to erupt in barbarism during the last year of his life.

## The Emperor's Tomb

*The Emperor's Tomb* first appeared in 1938, a year before *The Tale of the 1002nd Night*. Nonetheless, it, rather than the latter, should be regarded as Roth's last novel. For Roth was still working on *The Emperor's Tomb* when, after repeated delays, he finally submitted *The Tale of the 1002nd Night* for printing—but then urged his Dutch publisher, De Gemeenschap, to withhold it. Indeed, both books were published late, owing in good part to Roth's harried personal situation and, linked with it, his nettlesome negotiations with the publisher. In pushing to have *The Emperor's Tomb* printed before *The Tale of the 1002nd Night,* Roth argued that political events in Austria had made it particularly timely, whereas the plot of *The Tale of the 1002nd Night,* set in the previous century, had diminished in significance.[6] He expressly viewed *The Emperor's Tomb* as a sequel to *The Radetzky March,* which had appeared six years earlier when he was still able to publish in Germany. The fact that Roth introduces the central figure of *The Emperor's Tomb,* Franz Ferdinand Trotta, as an untitled, middle-class cousin of the protagonist of *The Radetzky March,* Carl Joseph von Trotta, provides the most immediate connection to the earlier work. Beyond the family relationship, however, Roth also incorporated prominent motifs and themes from *The Radetzky March* into the novel, although with significant shifts in meaning; and while *The Radetzky March* concludes with the death of the emperor Franz Joseph in 1916, the plot of *The Emperor's Tomb* continues the story of the Trottas and Austria into the 1930s. Above all, it is the Austrian theme that intrinsically links the two books.

As his first working title for the novel Roth chose "Ein Mann sucht sein Vaterland" (A Man Seeks His Fatherland). In addition to conveying the theme of his story, the descriptive image, as Roth surely knew, aptly characterized the greater part of his fictional work and the entirety of his personal life. In later correspondence with the publisher, he called the work "Der Kelch des Lebens" (The Cup of Life), before finally settling on the more starkly symbolic title, *The Emperor's Tomb.*[7] Originally, too, he wrote the novel in the third person, but then reworked it into a first-person narrative, perhaps to lend his plot greater immediacy. Set mainly in Vienna, the story begins in April 1913, fifteen months before the outbreak of World War I, in which Carl Joseph von Trotta sacrificed his life, and it ends in Vienna in mid-March 1938, just after Hitler's troops march into Austria and annex the country to the Third Reich. In a letter to De Gemeenschap, Roth himself proposed text for the brochure that would publicize the novel; he had intended it, he writes, as a "portrayal of the end of the last Austrian Reich." "By narrating private fates," Roth explained further, he was likewise recounting "the frightful death of the last corner of freedom in central Europe, the devouring of Austria by Prussia."[8]

At the start of the novel, Franz Ferdinand Trotta describes his relationship to the ennobled branch of the family by briefly retelling the story of the Hero of Solferino. The novel's final episode distills into a few poignant images the end of independent Austria and, with it, the last branch of the Trotta family. It reverberates with the futility of Trotta's existence and the demise of an age in the history of central Europe. A month after the death of his beloved mother, Trotta is pictured sitting alone in the darkness of his habitual Vienna coffee house after its Jewish owner, sensing Austria's imminent catastrophe, has closed its doors for the last time. Trotta then rises and steps aimlessly into the deserted nocturnal streets. Bereft of his mother and deserted by his wife, Elizabeth, who has gone off with her lesbian lover, he no longer knows where to turn. After a short while, his path leads him to the Capucian Crypt in the heart of the city and therewith to the concluding scene of the novel:

> The Kapuzinergruft, where my emperors lay buried in iron sarcophagi, was shut. The Capuchin brother came towards me and asked: "What do you want?"
>
> "I want to visit the sarcophagus of my Emperor, Franz Joseph," I replied.
>
> "God bless you!" said the brother and blessed me with his crucifix.
>
> "Long live the Emperor," I cried.
>
> "Psst," said the brother.
>
> So where could I go now, I, a Trotta?[9]

As the traditional burial place of the House of Habsburg, the Capucian Crypt is saturated with history. At the time of the Anschluss, in its sheer physical presence the building would suffice, in Trotta's understanding, to embody the end of Austria. For him, that is, the existence of the Austrian Republic that succeeded the monarchy is inseparable from the historical heritage of the Habsburgs. What fosters the convergence of image and idea in the concluding lines, however, is Roth's integration of Trotta's personal story with the historicity of the site. His despairing question, spoken to himself, makes clear that only an Austrian of his monarchist persuasions—shared by author Roth—could so intensely experience the finality symbolized in the crypt. His lonely steps through the streets of the Inner City are thus transformed into the hopeless search for the homeland that has already ceased to exist politically.

Like his cousin in *The Radetzky March,* Franz Ferdinand is hampered by his inability to cope with the everyday demands of his personal life. In like measure, he bears the melancholy of the son who is unable to assume the weighty heritage of his forebears. More consequential for the persuasiveness of the novel, however, are the differences between the two. Carl Joseph's search for an Austria in which he could feel rooted arose from his inner depths and defined his entire existence. The powerful longing to join himself with his family origins harbored within it, in sublimated form, the national aspirations of Austria's non-German minorities, which finally led to the dissolution of the monarchy. Franz Ferdinand's own search for his Austrian homeland, however, lacks this sort of convincing psychological or spiritual motivation. Nor is it deeply embedded in the novel's narrative structure. Driven by the feeling of being lost in his time, a feeling that typifies his entire Vienna circle—much as it did that of Arnold Zipper in Roth's earlier novel of the post–World War I generation—Franz Ferdinand seeks in vain after a security he cannot clearly define. Whether he pursues it in the form of friendship with his male peers or love or the warmth of his parental home, it constantly eludes him. Even at the end of the novel, when Austria is faced for the second time with national extinction and Franz Ferdinand's longing for a home is most powerfully stirred, both the source of his longing and its goal remain intangible.

We learn, to be sure, that Franz Ferdinand Trotta is bound by the last will and testament of his rebellious Slovenian, yet loyally Austrian, father to pursue the latter's dream of a "Slav monarchy under the rule of the Habsburgs" and "a joint monarchy of Austrians, Hungarians and Slavs" (*ET* 8–9). Named by his father after the slain archduke and heir to the throne, he will never forget this charge; yet, it never ripens within him as a political persuasion or call to action.[10] Rather, it is Trotta's rejection of the society and its values, to which he returns after military service, that underlies his fidelity to the past. Only at the end of the novel, when he stands helplessly before the Capucian Crypt, the eloquent symbol of his country's end, does this Austrian devotion assume form as a poetically transformed confession of allegiance.

Like *The Radetzky March*, *The Emperor's Tomb* is inspired thematically by the retrogressive utopian vision of Old Austria that Roth cherished. For all of its flaws, the multiethnic empire came to represent in his eyes, and in the eyes of countless other loyal Austrians, the possibility of an all-embracing, protective, and nourishing homeland, a possibility, moreover, that was capable of renewal. In *The Emperor's Tomb*, Roth extended his belief in the viability of the Austrian Idea, which he passionately championed in *The Radetzky March*, to the Second Austrian Republic. Although Franz Ferdinand has inherited the belief in this idea from his father, once again it is the ardent Austrian Count Chojnicki, resurrected from the earlier novel, now as a member of Franz Ferdinand's coffee house circle, who vehemently proclaims it.

As in *The Radetzky March*, too, it is Chojnicki who foretells the approaching extinction of Austria; and again, the force that dooms Chojnicki's homeland is nationalism. In *The Emperor's Tomb*, however, Roth's familiar thesis undergoes a notable transformation. Chojnicki no longer argues that it was the ethnic minorities with their nationalism who destroyed the monarchy. Condemned in *The Radetzky March* as idolaters, they are now transformed into a force that affirms and upholds Austria's existence. Instead, it is the Pangermanic Austrians whom Chojnicki excoriates. During the time of the monarchy, Chojnicki charges, they blinded themselves to the fact that the peoples of the borderlands were vital for the continued existence of the empire. After 1918, he contends, it was the Austro-Germans who again wantonly betrayed the still viable ideal of a supranational homeland for all of Austria's peoples:

[I]t is the Slovenes, the Poles and Galicians from Ruthenia, the kaftan-clad Jews from Boryslaw, the horse traders from the Bacska, the Moslems from Sarajevo, the chestnut roasters from Mostar who sing our national anthem, "Gott erhalte." But the German students from Brünn and Eger, the dentists, barbers' assistants, pharmacists and art photographers from Linz, Graz and Knittelfeld, the goitred creatures from the Alpine valleys, they all sing "Die Wacht am Rhein." Austria will perish at the hands of the Nibelungen fantasy, gentlemen! Austria's essence is not to be central, but peripheral. Austria is not to be found in the Alps, where you can find edelweiss, chamois and gentians but never a trace of the double eagle. The body politic of Austria is nourished and constantly replenished from the Crown Lands. (*ET* 17)

The fervor of this pronouncement contrasts starkly with Franz Ferdinand

Trotta's melancholy acceptance of his own, personal fate. Altogether, in fact, the reader misses in this Trotta, burdened though he is, the intense inner conflict that in *The Radetzky March* drove his cousin to his symbolically transfigured death.

Chojnicki's prophetic exhortation likewise underscores the decadence of his listeners, all of them young idle members of Viennese upper-class society. The reader might also expect that, as a declaration of Roth's own credo, the count's pronouncement will somehow influence the course of the narrative; yet it remains so conspicuously without motivating effect that it appears misplaced and artificial. The fact that Chojnicki's words fail to affect Trotta, even to elicit a commentary from him, points in particular to a double flaw. One is the superficiality of Trotta's Austrian sentiments; the other is a narrative weakness of the novel: in the last analysis, *The Emperor's Tomb* lacks an overarching, unifying theme.

Like his cousin, Franz Ferdinand finds himself drawn to Sipolje, his ancestral home in Slovenia. But while Carl Joseph feels himself driven to reforge the links with his family's Slavic past, what moves Franz Ferdinand is a shallow romantic disposition, to which the family history merely lends an individual twist. Instead of Sipolje, however, circumstances take him, as they once did his cousin, to the "northern sister of Slovenia," Galicia. There, in the town of Zlotogrod, he will stay with the Jewish coachman Manes Reisiger, who earlier had sought him out in Vienna in order to gain help in enrolling his son at the music conservatory. In anticipation of the trip, Franz Ferdinand, along with his equally enthusiastic friends, endows the distant town with qualities that are foreign to it but that satisfy their own romantic fantasies—much in the way that the elder Trotta in *The Radetzky March* had painted for himself an exotic, adventurous image of Carl Joseph's eastern garrison town before his visit there. In contrast, however, the Zlotogrod Roth pictures fails entirely to reveal the portents of Austria's downfall that in *The Radetzky March* lend the Galician borderland its narrative significance. In the eyes of Franz Ferdinand, the treacherous, uncannily threatening swamps of *The Radetzky March* are "luscious and benevolent," just as the entire region gives "an impression of courage and freedom from care" (*ET* 40). Only much later does Franz Ferdinand realize that he and the officers stationed in Zlotogrod had blinded themselves to the harbingers of death that surrounded them.

That Roth also succumbed to the same romanticizing tendencies as his central figure becomes apparent in his sentimentally overdone depiction of the unlikely friendship between Franz Ferdinand Trotta, his Slovenian cousin, the itinerant chestnut roaster Joseph Branco, and their mutual Jewish friend Manes Reisiger. Because Roth so idealized this friendship, the narrative intent that underlies it becomes patently clear: On the periphery of the monarchy, eulogized by Chojnicki as the life-giving heart of the monarchy, the idea of Austria as a supranational homeland has preserved its vitality. Through their bond, the German-Austrian Trotta, the Slovenian Branco, and the *Ostjude* Reisiger testify to the continued viability of this idea. Indeed, Chojnicki himself epitomizes Branco's trade as "[s]ymbolic for the old Monarchy" since he could ply it in all of the crownlands without need of a visa (*ET* 140). Spoken by Chojnicki— in the new novel, too, a convincingly drawn figure—the homey parallel rings true. But when Trotta, echoing Chojnicki, recites a veritable catalog of faithful Austrians—among others, the "gypsies of the Puszta," "the Swabian tobacco growers from the Bacska," "the Osman Sibersna," "the horse traders from the Hanakei in Moravia," and "the millers and coral dealers of Podolia" (*ET* 61)— he comes across as a talking puppet on the knee of author Roth.

The thrust of Roth's narrative suggests that it will be the prime task of the First Austrian Republic, arisen from the ruins of the First World War, to renew the concept of supranationality and give it concrete existence. Instead, however, the country falls victim to Pangermanism. The historical and political events from the time of the monarchy and the First Austrian Republic to, following the four years of the Fatherland Front dictatorship, Austria's incorporation into the Third Reich form the background to the novel. In unfolding its plot, Roth translated them into the personal tragedy of his protagonist.

On Christmas Eve 1918 Franz Ferdinand Trotta returns from war imprisonment in Siberia to an Austria that has been shorn of its former crownlands and thus turned into a center without a periphery. As he walks from the station through the gloomy streets of Vienna, he recalls his father's dream of a monarchy of Austrians, Hungarians, and Slavs under the Habsburgs. He makes a detour past the Capucian Crypt, spies the sentry before it and reflects: "What had he still to guard? The sarcophagi? Remembrance? History?" (*ET* 93). The questions that the site awakens in Trotta reflect the forlornness of his own existence, but this will achieve definitive expression only at the very end of the novel.

Because Franz Joseph was the last of the Habsburg rulers to be buried in the Capucian Crypt, in the new Austrian Republic the site has become historical; it exists, that is, without a vital function. For just this reason and because the death of the emperor has sealed the monarchist Trotta's personal fate, the imperial crypt, paradoxically, can claim a living presence for him. The same diminution that Roth portrays in the macrocosm of Austrian history is reflected in the microcosm of Trotta's own life. His steadily worsening personal situation goes hand in hand with the progressive reduction of his close surroundings. The restaurant in which he once felt securely at home has now become the favorite of his profiteering father-in-law, who represents the alien values of the postwar period. Sitting with strangers, being served by unfamiliar waiters, Trotta feels "stranger than a stranger" (*ET* 102). Similarly, he will become estranged from his parental home, which after his father's death harbors for him the warmth, security, and immutable order of his mother's love. Soon, however, financial distress leads to its conversion into a pension. And when his wife abandons him, his beloved mother dies, and he is forced to send his young son to live with a friend in Paris, his loss of home becomes complete. Recalling the nighttime walks of his youth with a friend through the streets of Vienna, he says: "The houses in which we lived seemed to us to be crypts or, at best, refuges" (*ET* 151). As though anticipating the end, Trotta's metaphor of the crypt reflects the emptiness and futility of his life and, as the first-person plural reference shows, that of an entire generation. Roth's readers will know it as the unsuspecting generation that was sent to fight in the First World War and, if they survived it, then struggled to find their place in the new, materialistic society that awaited them on their return.

Trotta's last refuge is the coffee house. But there, too, he finds himself isolated, "extra-territorial among the living" (*ET* 152). On the evening with which the novel ends, a young man appears in the uniform of the Austrian Nazi party and announces a new German people's rule. When the Jewish proprietor leaves Trotta behind as the sole remaining patron and lets down the outside shutters, the transformation of the coffee house into a crypt is complete. At this point, Roth's protagonist has neither a present nor a future; like the Capucian Crypt, his history belongs to the past. As he walks toward the tomb, with inexorable irony his personal story converges with that of Austria. For Trotta, Austria now exists solely in the concrete and, at the same time, symbolic form of the Capucian Crypt. There remains only the question that resonates without answer at the novel's end: "So where could I go now, I, a Trotta?" (*ET* 157). But while Trotta's forsakenness reverberates movingly in these words, on at least two counts the artistic achievement of the novel falls well short of *The Radetzky March.* Just as Roth failed in *The Emperor's Tomb* convincingly to illuminate the political factors that led to the downfall of the empire and the First Republic, he also failed to locate the source of his protagonist's misfortunes in a way that would cogently link them with the larger historical symbolism of the imperial crypt. The clear accomplishment of the novel, on the other hand, rests in Roth's ability to capture the atmosphere of finality that grows ever more dense as Trotta's story proceeds and finds eloquent expression at its end as his words resound into a void.

# CHAPTER 7

# Riddles of a Torn Existence

The real and encompassing truth of Franz Ferdinand Trotta's words at the end of *The Emperor's Tomb*—"So where could I go now, I, a Trotta?"—is Roth's own. After the Anschluss he, like Trotta, had nowhere to go; but for him this was a reality that issued from the sum of his entire life. The truth of Roth's end was that of his beginning: the writer without a homeland had never possessed one. From the time of his birth in Brody, homelessness had been his portion. Despite the efforts of his anxious mother to wrap the fatherless boy in her protective mantle, or perhaps because her efforts were so zealous, throughout his formative years he lacked the natural warmth and security of a family life. Although he was twenty-eight years old when his mother died, his preserved correspondence contains not one letter to her, and only once does he refer to her in a way that can be called affectionate.[1] Of his absent father he learned little and could replace him only with images of his own making. As he grew to young manhood and looked to make his way in the world, he rejected the choices that Brody offered him: Jewish traditionalist, Polish, or Zionist. His birthplace held no future for an aspiring German writer, and he left it early for the promise of Imperial Vienna. There he launched his literary career, but it would be mistaken to regard him as a Viennese writer—in the sense that his older contemporaries Arthur Schnitzler or Peter Altenberg were, both of whose lives and work were inseparably linked with the city.[2] In his novels and early feuilletons, Roth brilliantly captured Vienna's multifaceted ambiance, but for him it was the periphery of Austria, the crownlands, above all his native Galicia, that embodied Austria and that he lastingly brought to life in his novels; and it was this accomplishment that secured him his place as a great Austrian novelist in twentieth-century German literature.

Despite Roth's thorough Viennese acculturation, the result of a persistent effort, it would likewise be mistaken to see him as an assimilated Viennese. To be sure, countless others who migrated to Vienna before and after him succeeded over time in offsetting the encumbrances of their provincial backgrounds; Roth, however, remained ever burdened emotionally by his Galician-Jewish origins. The confinements he had sought to leave behind in Brody were more than those peculiar to a backwater endlessly distant from the cultural hub of the empire.

Although modernity had also made its inroads among the Jews of Brody, an ancient, all-embracing ethnic and religious heritage present in Roth's own boyhood home sufficed to stamp him—and others like him—as an alien in an epoch of virulent nationalism. Roth arrived in Vienna determined to erase the imprint of his Galician-Jewish birth; yet in cosmopolitan Vienna too—indeed, until the end of his life—Brody refused to yield its innermost claims on him. Just as the town suffused his work as a physical and emotional presence in ways both clear and hidden, it also accounts for the lifelong masquerade of identity that makes his figure so unhappy and yet engrossing.

Roth's funeral in Paris on 30 May 1939, three days after his death, has been described in detail by his biographer David Bronsen.[3] In its dissonances it mirrored the incongruities of personality and worldview that had marked Roth's entire mature existence. Among the many mourners at the cemetery were delegates from the conservative Liga für das Geistige Österreich (League for Austrian Culture). They laid down a wreath with the colors of the First Austrian Republic. Also at the graveside were Austrian legitimists from the circle of pretender to the throne Otto von Habsburg, in whose name a wreath was placed to honor Roth as a "loyal defender of the Monarchy." Confronting this group, the Prague-born journalist Egon Erwin Kisch, representing the communist Schutzverband Deutscher Schriftsteller (Association for the Protection of German Writers), tossed a bouquet of red carnations into the open grave. Just as delicate was the confrontation between the Catholics and Jews. The former had pressed for a Catholic burial, but lacking proof that Roth had actually converted, agreed to a "modified" religious ceremony. With that, Roth's Jewish friends, who insisted that he had remained a Jew, abstained from reciting the traditional mourner's prayer. Faced with the Catholic priest, however, several of them stepped to the grave and, reportedly, began praying in Hebrew.

As numerous recollections confirm, the large presence at Roth's gravesite attested to the fascination that his personality had exercised on all who knew him, to the admiration that his gifts as a writer commanded, and to his unyielding opposition to Nazism. Of the contradictions that their mixed company presented, some were genuine, others superficial. In one instance it was personal friendship with Roth, in another literary ties, in still another political affinities, real or perceived, that had brought so many persons of varied backgrounds and sometimes conflicting loyalties together.[4] Certainly, Egon Erwin Kisch rejected Roth's monarchism as decidedly as Roth rejected Kisch's communism. What united the two, besides an instinctive liking for one another, was their fight against Hitler. And while it is true that after the First World War Roth had aimed harsh criticism against the First Republic, calling it, for example, "a brand-new state . . . miserably patched together with old Imperial-Royal boards,"[5] once the existence of the republic was endangered both from within and without, he defended it, and continued to as a cofounder of the League for Austrian Culture in the fall of 1938. At bottom, however, the Austria he was defending had long since passed from existence. It existed solely as his own inner vision, as the idealized Austria of the "good Franz Joseph," and sprang from Roth's longing for a rooted identity.

Even in his early socialist days, political acumen had not been Roth's strength, nor was he politically engaged. But the monarchist activism of his exile years, for all of its earnestness, was unrealistic in the extreme. The tensions between ideal and inexorable reality, which he had portrayed sublimely in *The Radetzky March* and with masterful irony in *The Tale of the 1002nd Night,* gave way amid the radical homelessness of exile to a politics of desperation—accompanied by reckless drinking. Old beyond his forty-five years, deathly sick, and spiritually despondent at the triumph of Hitler's pestilential ideology, like his friends Ernst Toller and Stefan Zweig, he could not have survived emigration to a foreign continent.[6] It was only in a restored monarchy, a resurrection of the Austrian universalist ideal, that the Galician Jew Roth could imagine a home for himself. It is this fantasy, born of longing and nourished by despair, that explains Roth's unlikely Habsburg legitimism; and more than anything else, it explains his repeated, and much debated, avowals of Catholicism.

For Roth and others who professed the Austrian Idea, Catholicism was the essence of Austrianism. In their hierarchical structure, which was seen as divinely ordained, and in their embodiment of a universalist order that transcended national and ethnic particularisms, Catholicism and Austrianism were one. As imperfectly as the idea may have been translated by the Habsburgs into political reality, the Jews of Austria above all others understood its blessings. For those who wished it—and as long as a benign rule held sway—they could be Austrians *and* Jews without inner conflict. Roth, however, was oppressed by his Jewish origins, and he wished for more. Already in his young years he wished to assimilate completely as an Austrian of German culture; and although this endeavor proved illusory, Catholicism was its indispensable social element. Roth's "conversion" was not one of ambition or convenience. Unlike Heinrich Heine in the century before him, Roth did not seek an academic career that would have been closed to him as a Jew; and unlike Gustav Mahler at the turn of his own century, he did not seek to direct a world-famous cultural institution, a position likewise blocked for a Jew.[7] What he sought, desperately and, in the end, futilely, was of this world, to be sure, but his whole existence depended on gaining it. Even as he clung to facets of his Jewish self, he sought release from its emotional burdens. This was perhaps his greatest paradox, but only in flight from the person he was could he overcome his homelessness, his status as an outsider, and achieve full acceptance as a German writer. In this existential regard, so he must have felt, the Catholic Church held out the chance for salvation.

The dispute that broke out among Roth's friends and associates over his religious identity and the form of his burial remains as unresolvable today as it was then. Those who appear to have known him best gave starkly conflicting witness; for each heated contention on the one side there is an equally persuasive rebuttal on the other.[8] Finally, however, respect for Roth's undoubtedly sincere public declarations of his Catholicism in articles and feuilletons should have sufficed to silence the debate—except that he himself fueled it persistently and in ways that even now make the matter a prime riddle of his life. As often as he disclosed to friends that he had been baptized, he just as often assured others that he had not. And while a baptismal certificate was in fact lacking, Hermann Kesten observed correctly, with reference to Roth, that true devotion to a belief needs nothing more to authenticate it.[9] In this light, it is hard to judge the significance of Roth's emphatic statement in a letter of 2 April 1936 to Stefan Zweig that he was "a believing *Ostjude,* from Radziwilow" (*BR* 465)—unless in Roth's understanding being both a Catholic and Jewish believer may have somehow been compatible.[10] Such imponderables aside, testimony from Roth's confidant in Paris, the Lithuanian-born journalist and Jewish educator Joseph Gottfarstein, compounds the question of Roth's faith in a way that borders on fiction itself. To Gottfarstein, Roth swore that his Catholicism was nothing but a ruse, intended to enhance his legitimist voice in Austrian aristocratic circles in Paris.[11] If this was true, it was surely the most bizarre role among the several that Roth played in his life. Yet in all of its extremity it would add only one more page to the tortured history of the "German-Jewish symbiosis" that never was.

From the time of Heinrich Heine to the end of Jewish community life in Germany and Austria under Nazism, it would be difficult, perhaps impossible, to find a Jewish writer or artist who at some point in his or her life was spared the conflict of German-Jewish identity. The most searing document of this conflict and its painful costs can be found in the memoir of the novelist Jakob Wassermann (1873–1934), *Mein Weg als Deutscher und Jude* (1921; My Life as German and Jew). In his key remarks of 1962, "Against the Myth of the German-Jewish Dialogue," Gershom Scholem called Wassermann's book "a true cry into the void that knew itself to be such."[12] Without doubt, it was also the cry of countless thousands of plain German Jews, who, unlike Wassermann, lived out their lives in relative obscurity. The impossibility of fully entering the community of the German nation because the Germans themselves denied them such entry, led individual Jewish men and women to responses as varied in form and intensity as the rejection they experienced. They span the gamut from resignation, bitterness, and helpless anger to heartbreak, and even suicide. Others sought to escape their dilemma by embracing political-ideological causes and beliefs, from socialist and communist universalism to Jewish nationalism in the form of Zionism.

Jewish self-hate, as the cultural philosopher Theodor Lessing (1872–1933) described it in his book by the same name, was the most pernicious psychological reaction of untold Jews to their rejection by German and Austrian society.[13] That such destructive feelings resonated powerfully in the life and work of many Jewish writers and thinkers, some renowned, others since forgotten, is well documented. Not always did it manifest itself so repellently and tragically as with the Viennese philosopher Otto Weininger (1880–1903) or the likewise Viennese cultural historian Arthur Trebitsch (1880–1927), both of whom Lessing placed at the center of his book.[14] Unable to overcome what he saw as the inherent curse of his Jewish birth, Weininger shot himself at the age of twenty-four, while Trebitsch, a truly pathological anti-Semite, descended into madness. Writing on the relationship of Franz Kafka and Karl Kraus to their Jewishness, Werner Kraft rightly said of Kraus that he "was as much against the Jews and Christians of his time as he was for the Jews and Christians of his time; he was for the world and saving the world." Yet, Kraus was not free, as Kraft claimed, of the "anti-Jewish complex" that at times emerges disturbingly in Kafka's diaries and letters.[15] Rather, Kraus's lifelong battle against the corrupt language and morality of Austrian bourgeois society bore unambiguous signs of the Jewish self-hatred with which Lessing charged him.[16] In significant contrast to Kraus, Kafka rejected his Jewishness because as an assimilated Jew of German education and culture he found himself wanting in Jewish substance—which he subsequently labored to acquire. As Kraft stresses, the values against which Kafka measured himself were neither those of Germanness nor Christianity but of Judaism itself, and this fact separates him most decisively of all from not only Weininger, but also from Wassermann and still others.[17]

More names could be added to the writers cited above. Observed in detail, their lives and work would show that the phenomenon of German-Jewish self-hate encompasses a broad and subtle range of expressions and intensities. In its "classic" form, however, it reflects a basic psychological pattern: Tormented by an unjust and irrevocable status as despised or, in better circumstances, barely tolerated outsiders, but unable to break free from it, these German Jews capitulated and rejected themselves. Reacting as the pariahs to which they were reduced, and as veritable anti-Semites, they turned their turbulent emotions inward against themselves and outward against the specter of *the* Jews and their imagined ruinous influence on the world. To this syndrome, Roth presents an unusual and perplexing variant. Nowhere do his novels and stories betray the familiar signs of German-Jewish self-hate. With some notable exceptions, his Jewish figures are portrayed sympathetically and sensitively, and often with deep affection. Mendel Singer in *Job,* as well as a host of secondary figures—among them Max Demant in *The Radetzky March,* Shemariah in *Tarabas,* and Manes Reisiger in *The Emperor's Tomb*—were clearly close to the author's heart. And the Jewish villains of Roth's fiction are no more villainous than others, nor does their evil derive from traits that are depicted as peculiar to Jews; treachery and violence in Roth's world are universal human vices. Yet the evidence of his private letters and journal contributions shows that he, too, was infected by the virus of German-Jewish self-hate, or a strain of it that might be better characterized as German-Jewish self-denial, which, however, often found hostile expression when projected outward.[18]

In part, Roth's effacement of his Galician birth may have been socially motivated, but taken together with other related obfuscations it betrays shame over his Jewish origins. Decidedly more questionable was the consistent masking of his father's Jewish identity, in effect a disavowal of his father and, as its intent, at least a partial disavowal of his own Jewishness. More than once in formal dealings he suppressed the fact of his Jewish birth entirely, misrepresenting himself as an Austrian Catholic. Yet with all this he frequently took it upon himself to speak in the name of the Jewish people—or rather the orthodox part of the Jewish people, which he regarded as the only genuine one. When he argued in his essay "Der Segen des ewigen Juden" (The Blessing of the Wandering Jew) that the Jews "were scattered among the nations in order to spread God's name,"[19] he could, in fact, find support for this notion in Hebrew Scripture and Jewish religious thought. He likewise stood within Jewish tradition when he maintained that it was God's will that the Jews suffer in their exile (*BR* 281). But the Jewish messianic idea which underlies these views is incompatible with the Christian messianism that Roth's declarations of Catholic belief imply. From the chapter "Vengeance is His" in *Antichrist,* it becomes clear, in fact, that Roth's understanding of Jewish exile is grounded in the Christian view of the triumph of the church over the synagogue and the Jews' mission to witness the truth of Christianity (*AC* 134–36). Assuming—no doubt, rightly—that the Zionist leader Chaim Weizmann would regard him politically as a "renegade," Roth protested in a letter of 14 August 1935 to Stefan Zweig: "I am more than happy to be a renegade, from Germans *and* Jews, and I am proud of it. *Thanks to this,* I am not a renegade from Christians and humankind" (*BR* 421). While the dichotomies

Roth suggests here permit various conclusions, his declaration clearly reveals the same anti-Jewish complex that surfaces in *Antichrist.*

More than once Roth conceded that political Zionism might be a practical necessity, but as a champion of Austrianism, he opposed the movement as a solution to the "Jewish Problem"—just as he opposed every form of nationalism. Yet his equation in a letter to Zweig— "A Zionist is a National Socialist, a Nazi is a Zionist" (*BR* 420)[20]—defies historical facticity to a degree that suggests a potent affect as its motivating force. Similarly, in a letter to Blanche Gidon, Roth identified the socialism of the French-Jewish political leader and parlamentarian Léon Blum with anti-Semitism, effectively branding Blum himself an anti-Semite. Beyond this, Roth argued that as the creators of socialism the Jews had brought about "the catastrophe of European culture," calling them "the true cradle of Hitler" (*BR* 406).[21] Like the parallel between Nazism and Zionism, this charge, too, is so strikingly at odds with historical objectivity that Roth's extreme cultural and political conservatism no longer suffices to explain it. Rather, the explicit content of such judgments and their heated pronouncement suggest that they, too, arise from an anti-Jewish complex deeply seated in Roth's torn self.

Despite these inner conflicts, Roth stands apart from other German-Jewish writers who reacted with self-hate or self-denial to what they felt was the disgrace of their Jewish birth. What separates him from them above all is his deep and abiding affection for the Jews of eastern Europe. Although he himself escaped the ostracism that was their lot, he knew the story firsthand of their social rejection by their western coreligionists. Seeking haven from destitution, pogroms, and the ravages of war, from the 1890s through World War I tens of thousands of traditional Jews from the Slavic lands fled to Vienna, Berlin, and other western cities where they formed distinct ethnic enclaves. Anxious lest their own painfully earned entry into German society be threatened by this large "alien" presence, established German Jewry responded in diverse ways. On the part of many there was scornful rejection of the émigrés and refugees; on the part of many more there was emotional ambivalence; on the part of others, the organized communities, there was active assistance, intended mainly to help their wanting brethren move on.[22] Roth's personal response was his book-essay *Juden auf Wanderschaft* (*The Wandering Jews*). In his foreword he states resoundingly that his book was not intended for readers "who disdain, contemn, hate, and harry the *Ostuden.*" He then describes the sort of reader he wishes:

> The author cherishes the foolish hope that there are still readers to whom one need not defend the *Ostjuden;* readers who have respect for pain, deep humanity, and the grime that accompanies suffering no matter where; west Europeans, who are not proud of their clean beds; who feel that they might

93

have much to gain from the east, und who perhaps know that great persons and great ideas come from Galicia, Russia, Lithuania, Rumania, but also useful persons (in the western sense), human beings who uphold and help to expand the firm structure of western civilization; readers who know that the *Ostjuden* are not just the pickpockets to whom that most despicable product of the western Europeans, the local news report, refers as "guests from the east." (*W* 3:293)

The opposition of eastern and western Europe runs as a theme throughout the book as Roth contrasts the empty, materialistic civilization of western Europe, with its assimilated Jewry, and the spiritual culture of the orthodox *Ostjuden*. In the west, Jews function as commercial middlemen; in the east, aside from their concentration in small trade, Jews work productively: as craftsmen and—what was almost unknown in the west—as proletarians and even as farmers. On the one hand, bourgeois comfort and self-satisfaction; on the other, despite restriction and deprivation, group vitality. In the west, the perfunctory rituals of the reform temple that pass as devotion; in the east the religiosity of the orthodox synagogue and house of prayer. Above all, Roth's portrayal extols the *authenticity* of Jewish life in the premodern shtetl in contrast to its deformations in the cities of the "progressive" west.

Along with Alfred Döblin, Arnold Zweig, and other contemporary German-language portrayers of east European Jewry, Roth, too, idealized his subject.[23] Except for the growing influence of Jewish nationalism and political Zionism—in his eyes western inventions—he largely neglects the forces of modernism that had already begun to tear at the social and religious fabric of the shtetl in the last quarter of the previous century. Perhaps the pronounced subjectivity of his book was determined strategically by his intent to defend the *Ostjuden* against their ostensibly more civilized western maligners; or perhaps its sources lay deeper in Roth's personality. Zweig, like many German Jews, first experienced traditional Jewry during his army service at the eastern front in World War I. Others, like Kafka, first encountered *Ostjuden* in the west, as refugees from the war. In 1924 Döblin traveled from Berlin to Poland to study them. Common to all three and still other German-Jewish writers of the time was the search for Jewish authenticity, which had been lost through the assimilatory attempts of earlier generations.[24] Roth, however, had grown to maturity in the very midst of those *Ostjuden* who for his fellow writers were an unexpected discovery. But when he left his native grounds, he intended the break to be for good.

Except for a short visit to his mother in Brody in 1918, Roth never returned to his birthplace—neither during his trip to Poland as a reporter in 1928 nor during his lecture tour there in 1937. But *The Wandering Jews* meant, in fact, an emotional return to the origins that he had long taken pains to obscure. Nine years after his departure for the west, he confesses that assimilation can never fully succeed and he laments even the attempt to assimilate.[25] While Jews may suffer scorn and persecution in their separateness, he explains, God's reward awaits them (*W* 3:308–9). Here there is still no hint of the Christian doctrine that in *Antichrist* and elsewhere negates Roth's seemingly strong Jewish allegiance.[26] Even in his lengthy discussion of Zionism the vehement tone of rejection that was to typify his later pronouncements is absent. Rather, Roth demonstrates understanding for the Zionist rationale, but opposes to it his view of the Jews as a universal community of faith, one that defies the western concept of nationhood and the nation state.

Nowhere in *The Wandering Jews* does his reverence for the Jews of the shtetl and their religiosity express itself so unmistakably as when he describes their observance of the Day of Atonement, Yom Kippur. With utmost sympathy and eloquence he evokes the solemnity of the holy day, and depicts with almost tangible awe an assembly of believers joined as one in the fear of God and the zeal to reach Him with their penitential prayers. The adjective "all" rings through his description with an insistence that admits no exceptions: "All of the fathers now bless their children. All of the women now weep before the silver candlesticks. All friends embrace. All enemies beg one another for forgiveness. . . . Candles now burn for all of the dead. Others burn for all of the living" (*W* 3:316). Roth surrenders himself so completely to the spirit of communal observance that he nearly disappears as an observer. Could his subjects have read his tribute to their piety, they would have recognized themselves in it without doubt—just as they would have recognized themselves in his account of their workaday existence.

Seven years after *The Wandering Jews* (and four years after he had paid homage to east European Jewry in the novel *Job*), Roth incorporated his Yom Kippur description virtually unchanged into *Antichrist*—although the new context was wholly antithetical to Jewish belief. In the unlikely case that the book would have found orthodox readers—and for Roth the orthodox were the sole true believers—they would have assuredly denounced its author as a renegade from his faith and people. How Roth would have responded can only be a matter for speculation. In the throes of his exile years, the professing Catholic repeatedly vowed to enter a monastery, and at the same time adamantly claimed for himself the identity of an *Ostjude,* which he had consciously suppressed. Yet he had written in *The Wandering Jews* that this was impossible, that the assimilationist's effort "to flee from the sad community of the persecuted was an attempt to reconcile conflicting forces that cannot be reconciled" (*W* 3:308). Of Roth's varied paradoxes, this one was the most consequential for his personal and literary existence.

Faced with such riddles of personality and persuasion, David Bronsen suggests that Roth uprooted himself psychologically when he abandoned the cultural world of the shtetl in order to assimilate as a "westerner." The "psychic split" that he lived with thereafter resulted in "a deep underlying shame" which caused him to suppress the Jewish components of his identity. Because these nonetheless asserted themselves, Roth was forced to "compartmentalize" the opposing aspects of his being, now representing one, now the other.[27] Much evidence speaks for the validity of this interpretation, yet Roth's figure is so bewilderingly complex that it, too, leaves primary questions untouched. Rather than succumb to self-denial and an insistent anti-Jewish complex, why was Roth unable naturally to accept his origins and by this act perhaps make a whole of his life and his writing? Western prejudices and the ill consequences of assimilation that he deplored among modern Jewry were real enough, but there were also real attempts by German and Austrian Jews to overcome them. Martin Buber, too, as he himself affirmed, was an *Ostjude*—of Galician background, moreover—yet he found his way, within the German language, to Jewish spiritual renewal, and others in Prague, Berlin, and Vienna followed him on this path. To be sure, it led many of them to Zionism, but the example of Buber's Frankfurt friend and collaborator Franz Rosenzweig (1886–1929) shows that Zionism was not its inevitable outcome: instead of assimilation, Rosenzweig sought a synthesis of the German and Jewish spirit, and his influence was strong. The Berlin cultural critic Walter Benjamin (1892–1940) was yet another seminal thinker who struggled with the polarities of German-Jewish identity. Although his restless spirit left him adrift among contending solutions, he, too, never exhibited the symptoms of German-Jewish self-rejection. In this regard, for reasons that elude discernment, Roth failed.

To delve deeper than Bronsen into the enigmas that Roth presents would be the valid task of a Freudian biography. Given especially Roth's "ghost" father and his overly possessive mother, the classical family conflict must have been powerfully present in his formative years. Indeed, considering that Roth's mother was named Maria, his statement in a letter that he was born "under the sign of Virgo, with whom my first name Joseph stands in some vague relationship" (*BR* 165), nearly begs for a Freudian reading. In the end, however, the value of the insights gained would be offset by the reductionism that the psychoanalytic process by its nature entails. What would inevitably become lost is the poetry of an individual existence, the drama of hopes fulfilled and more often defeated, of transient joys and lasting sorrows, lived out by ordinary people everywhere, but always bearing the imprint of a personality exchangeable with no other; and it would tell us nothing, because it cannot, about Roth's narrative genius. Decisive though Roth's family circumstances surely were, the story of his personal and artistic existence was defined, too, by the objective forces of history, and Roth's defining historical experience was Imperial Austria in its irreversible decline. But it became that for him only in the early 1930s, when the monarchy of Franz Joseph was no more than a nostalgic memory and its successor state, the First Republic, was increasingly threatened by economic instability and social and political strife. Beset by misfortune and homeless as never before, the despairing Roth now turned to the past and in his crowning work, *The Radetzky March,* he resurrected Old Austria in order that he might mourn its passing.

With the singular exception of *The Tale of the 1002nd Night,* Roth's novels in exile fall below the pinnacle achievements of *The Radetzky March* and *Job.* But amid the ordeals of this period his creative powers did not lessen. On the contrary, despite patently weak books like *The Ballad of the Hundred Days, Weights and Measures,* and *The Emperor's Tomb,* he remained a genial storyteller to the end. Both *Confession of a Murderer* and *Tarabas* have lost nothing of their human appeal and artistic vitality and will continue to gratify readers through their inventive plots, vivid characters and settings, and thematic intensity. The most eloquent testimony to Roth's enduring narrative gifts, however, is *The Tale of the 1002nd Night.* That Roth was able to wrest this masterful work, lighthearted and tragic at once, from the misery of his last years, must be seen as a triumph of his narrative genius. But it was a triumph from which he could have taken no reward. Its damnatory last words, spoken by the waxwork artisan Tino Percoli, were Roth's hopeless protest against the evil of Nazism that Germany now embodied and that threatened to engulf all of Europe. The qualities that had always mattered most for Roth, "heart, conscience, passion, emotion, and decency," Percoli laments, had been extinguished everywhere, what people wanted were "monsters" (*TN* 261). Roth knew that his hopes for Europe's rescue from the Nazi pestilence were illusory, and he died without consolation. Of the many tributes that were paid him after his death, the most fitting may have come from his Austrian compatriot and admired friend Alfred Polgar. In the exile journal *Die österreichische Post,* on 1 July 1939, Polgar wrote: "The homeland, in which his name may not be mentioned today, will name him with deep respect when it will again be possible there to call vile what is vile and noble what is noble."[28] In books that will endure through the grace of their language, form, and imagination, Joseph Roth condemned what is coarse and cold in the human heart and society, and upheld "heart, conscience, passion, emotion, and decency." This is his legacy to the present and future.

# Notes

## Chapter 1: Introduction

1. For a highly informative analysis of Roth's literary reception, see Margarete Willerich-Tocha, *Rezeption als Gedächtnis: Studien zur Wirkung Joseph Roths* (Frankfurt am Main: Peter Lang, 1984); for the period under discussion, see especially 144–50.

2. I am indebted for these summary remarks to the definitive introductory study by Alexander Stephan, *Die deutsche Exilliteratur 1933–1945* (Munich: Verlag C. H. Beck, 1979), chaps. 1 and 5.

3. *Joseph Roth. Leben und Werk: Ein Gedächtnisbuch,* ed. Hermann Linden (Cologne: Verlag Gustav Kiepenheuer, 1949).

4. Hermann Kesten, ed., *Werke in drei Bänden,* 3 vols. (Cologne and Berlin: Kiepenheuer and Witsch, 1956).

5. *Romane, Erzählungen, Aufsätze* (Cologne and Berlin: Kiepenheuer and Witsch, 1964).

6. Hermann Kesten, ed., *Werke. Neue erweiterte Ausgabe in vier Bänden,* 4 vols. (Cologne: Kiepenheuer and Witsch, 1975–1976). In 1989–1991, a third, further expanded edition of the *Werke* was published in six volumes: vols. 1–3, *Das journalistische Werk* (The Journalistic Works), ed. Klaus Westermann; vols. 4–6, *Romane und Erzählungen* (Novels and Stories), ed. Fritz Hackert. Unless otherwise noted, all references in the text to the *Werke* will follow the edition of 1975–1976, which will be cited parenthetically as W, with volume and page number; translations will be my own.

7. See Hugo von Hofmannsthal, "Die Österreichische Idee," in *Reden und Aufsätze 2, Gesammelte Werke* (Frankfurt am Main: S. Fischer, 1979), 454–58. The Italian Germanist Claudio Magris criticized the unrealistic conception of Austria, which Roth and other writers shared with Hofmannsthal, pointedly terming it "the Habsburg Myth." See Claudio Magris, *Der habsburgische Mythos in der österreichischen Literatur,* trans. Madeleine von Pasztory (Salzburg: O. Müller, 1966).

8. "The Bust of the Emperor," in *Hotel Savoy. Fallmerayer the Stationmaster. The Bust of the Emperor,* trans. John Hoare (Woodstock, N.Y.: Overlook Press, 1986), 157–58. Subsequent references to the story will be cited parenthetically in the text after the initials BE. This practice will be followed for all references in the text to Roth's work. See list of abbreviations.

9. In the English translation, Morstin's words echo John 14:2. The Martin Luther

Bible reads: "In meines Vaters Hause sind viele Wohnungen." The King James Version reads: "In my Father's house there are many mansions." Finally, the New Revised Standard Version reads: "In my Father's house there are many dwelling places." Although Roth's German text ("ein großes Haus mit vielen Türen und vielen Zimmern") and its English translation depart somewhat from all three, the source is easily recognizable.

10. Like all others who undertake to write on Joseph Roth, I am deeply indebted to the unsurpassable biography by David Bronsen, *Joseph Roth: Eine Biographie* (Cologne: Kiepenheuer and Witsch, 1974). References to it with page number will follow parenthetically in the text under the initials *DB*. A late and highly welcome complement to Bronsen's biography is the posthumously published memoir by Roth's close friend, the Galician-born novelist Soma Morgenstern (1890–1976), *Joseph Roths Flucht und Ende: Erinnerungen* (Lüneburg: zu Klampen, 1994). A third invaluable source of information on Roth's life and literary career is the voluminous collection of his letters, *Briefe 1911–1939,* ed. Hermann Kesten (Cologne: Kiepenheuer and Witsch, 1970). References to it will follow parenthetically in the text after the initials *BR*. A further, handy source of information is the catalog that accompanied the comprehensive 1979 Roth exhibition in Frankfurt: *Joseph Roth 1894–1939. Eine Ausstellung der Deutschen Bibliothek Frankfurt am Main,* ed. Brita Eckert and Werner Berthold, 2nd rev. ed. (Frankfurt am Main: Buchhändler-Vereinigung, 1979). References to this source will follow parenthetically in the text after the abbreviation *KAT*.

11. The first Roth scholar accurately to locate Szwaby / Schwabendorf as the neighborhood of the railroad station within the town of Brody itself, rather than to identify it as a nearby village, was Fritz Hackert. See his contribution "Joseph Roth" in *Deutsche Dichter des 20. Jahrhunderts,* ed. Hartmut Steinecke (Berlin: Erich Schmidt Verlag, 1996), 363.

12. *The Radetzky March,* trans. Joachim Neugroschl (Woodstock, N.Y.: Overlook Press, 1995), 129.

13. See the splendid photo and text volume on Roth's life and work by Heinz Lunzer and Victoria Lunzer-Talos, *Joseph Roth: Leben und Werk in Bildern* (Cologne: Kiepenheuer and Witsch, 1994), 30–35.

14. According to Soma Morgenstern (see note 10), less can be claimed for Roth's proficiency in Polish.

15. Interview with Keun in David Bronsen, *Joseph Roth: Eine Biographie,* 492. Irmgard Keun, at twenty-one, created a sensation with her first novel, *Gilgi, eine von uns* (1931). In her exile novel, *Nach Mitternacht* (1937), she relates the everyday experiences of a young woman during the early Nazi years. In *Kind aller Länder* (1938) she portrays Roth's end in lightly masked form from the perspective of a young girl. The tensions of her relationship with the emotionally volatile Roth led to their breakup early in 1938. Although she continued to publish after 1945 she was unable to match her earlier successes.

16. Robert Musil, *The Man without Qualities,* trans. Sophie Wilkens (New York: Alfred A. Knopf, 1995) 1:180.

17. Jakob Klein-Haparash, "Interview mit sich selbst," *Die Welt der Literatur,* 24 November 1966, 18.

18. See C. A. Maccartney, *The Habsburg Empire, 1790–1918* (New York: The Macmillan Company, 1969); also Antony Polonsky, "A Failed Pogrom: The Demonstrations in Lwów, June 1929" in *The Jews of Poland between Two World Wars,* ed. Israel Gutman, et al. (Hanover: University Press of New England, 1989), 109–125.

19. See Norman Davies, "Ethnic Diversity in Twentieth-Century Poland" in *From Shtetl to Socialism: Studies from Polin,* ed. Antony Polansky (London and Washington: The Littman Library of Jewish Civilization, 1993), 240–41.

20. See respectively Otto Forst de Battaglia, "Der Wanderer auf einer Flucht zum tragischen Ende," *Wort in der Zeit* 3, no. 4 (April 1957): 39–43; David Bronsen, "The Jew in Search of a Fatherland: The Relationship of Joseph Roth to the Habsburg Monarchy," *The Germanic Review* 54, no. 2 (spring 1979): 54–61; and Hermann Kesten, "Joseph Roth: Auf der Flucht vor dem Nichts," *Der Monat* 5, no. 59 (1953): 473–77.

21. "Leipziger Prozeß gegen die Rathenau-Mörder," *Werke I. Das journalistische Werk 1915–1923,* ed. Klaus Westermann (Cologne: Kiepenheuer and Witsch, 1989), 872–88.

22. See Sidney Rosenfeld, "Joseph Roth and Austria: A Search for Identity," *Publications of the Leo Baeck Institute. Year Book XXXI* (London: Secker & Warburg, 1986), 455–64; see especially 456–57.

23. For a short, instructive introduction to the question of Austrian writers and politics in exile, with attention to Joseph Roth, see Ulrich Weinzierl, "Zur nationalen Frage—Literatur und Politik im österreichischen Exil" in *Exilliteratur 1933–1945,* ed. Wulf Koepke and Michael Winkler (Darmstadt: Wissenschaftliche Buchgesellschaft, 1989), 241–276.

24. "The Legend of the Holy Drinker," *Right and Left. The Legend of the Holy Drinker,* trans. Michael Hofmann (Woodstock, N.Y.: Overlook Press, 1986), 287.

## Chapter 2: The Early Work, 1923–1924

1. *The Spider's Web and Zipper and His Father,* trans. John Hoare (Woodstock, N.Y.: Overlook Press, 1989), 96. Further references will follow parenthetically in the text after the abbreviation *SW.*

2. Cf. Feuchtwanger's 1930 novel *Erfolg* or Döblin's 1935 novel *Pardon wird nicht gegeben.* In contrast to *Erfolg,* to be sure, the latter work concentrates more on its protagonist's personal story than on political developments—which, however, roll in the background as a dark presence. It should be kept in mind also that both Feuchtwanger and Döblin were already well-established authors when they published these works, whereas Roth was just starting out.

3. *Hotel Savoy. Fallmerayer the Stationmaster. The Bust of the Emperor,* trans. John Hoare (Woodstock, N.Y.: Overlook Press, 1986), 9. Further references will follow parenthetically in the text after the abbreviation *HS.*

4. "Kirche, Staat, Volk, Judentum" in *Der Jude und sein Judentum: Gesammelte Aufsätze und Reden* (Cologne: Joseph Melzer Verlag, 1963), 569.

5. *Rebellion,* trans. Michael Hofmann (New York: St. Martin's Press, 1999), 2. Further references will follow parenthetically in the text after the abbreviation *R.*

6. In a polemical essay of January 1924 titled "Sittlichkeit und Kriminalität" (Morality and Criminality), the Viennese satirist and cultural critic Karl Kraus (1874–1936) described a civil justice case that parallels Andreas Pum's in striking detail. In the previous summer, a Vienna district court had charged an invalid organ grinder, Heinrich Reinthaler, with insult to both a public official and a private citizen ("Amts- und Privatehrenbeleidigung"). Andreas Pum, as Roth indicates through a secondary character, will be faced with almost the same charge: insult to a public official (*W* 1:283). Like Reinthaler, Pum was prevented from appearing before the court because at the set time he was being detained by the police, and subsequently he was punished with the severe penalty of six weeks in prison (in Reinthaler's case it was three weeks). In both instances, the defendant's inability to distinguish between legal subtleties exacerbated his plight. In espousing the cause of the defendant, both Roth and Kraus exposed the heartlessness of the justice system and branded it itself as criminal. See Karl Kraus, *Die Fackel* 25, no. 640 (1924): 34–38. Without doubt, Roth found both the core motif and the theme for his novel in the case of Heinrich Reinthaler. While he could have learned of it from a newspaper report, he may just as well have discovered it in *Die Fackel.* Despite his insistence that he had never been able to suffer the famously contentious Karl Kraus, Roth knew *Die Fackel* and regarded Kraus as one of Austria's most significant writers. In an article of 1 March 1939 for the émigré journal *Die Österreichische Post* (Paris), Roth acknowledged that he had learned from Kraus's example (see *W* 4:748–49).

## Chapter 3: The Early Work, 1927–1929

1. For somewhat more detailed information on the relationship of the two series to one another, see *Werke,* 3:880.

2. "Juden auf Wanderschaft," *Werke,* 3:291–369. The English translation of this work, *The Wandering Jews* appeared when my book was nearing publication. All translations are thus my own.

3. Hemingway's *The Sun Also Rises* (1926) and Fitzgerald's *Tender Is the Night* (1934) are the two novels generally considered to portray most closely the inner crisis of the American "lost generation" following World War I and the European world in which its representatives sought to escape their personal conflicts. While the similarities of historical situation and psychological motivation are instructive, it should be noted that the theme of the expatriate common to the American novels appears in Roth's novels of this period in a related but basically different form: Roth's protagonists are not expatriates but rather extraterritorial. In this context, it should also be noted that, despite the affinities, there is no evidence to show that Roth knew these writers and their works. Nonetheless, in a feuilleton of 29 January 1928 in the *Frankfurter Zeitung,* "Der Amerikanismus im Literaturbetrieb" (Americanism in the Literary Market), without citing titles he rejected the 1920s American novel of social criticism as artistically inferior. The sole writer he

names—and exempts from his criticism as a "'European' exception"—is John Dos Passos (though here, too, Roth cites no titles). See *Werke* 4:221–223.

4. For a brief, informative introduction to *Neue Sachlichkeit,* see the corresponding entry in *Moderne Literatur in Grundbegriffen,* ed. Dieter Borchmeyer and Viktor Žmegač (Tübingen: Max Niemeyer Verlag, 1994), 319–26.

5. *Flight without End,* trans. David Le Vay and Beatrice Musgrave (Woodstock, N.Y.: Overlook Press, 1977) Further references will follow parenthetically in the text after the abbreviation *FE.*

6. See "Reise in Rußland" (Travels in Russia) in *Werke,* 3: 935–1008. The series first appeared in the *Frankfurter Zeitung* from 21 September 1926 to 18 / 19 January 1927.

7. *The Spider's Web* and *Zipper and His Father,* trans. John Hoare (Woodstock, N.Y.: Overlook Press, 1989), 239–40. Further references will follow parenthetically in the text after the abbreviation *ZF.* The Hoare translation contains a conspicuous omission, which I have corrected within square brackets in the text. Generally speaking, Roth was often less than well served in some of the early translations of his books. All the more welcome are the newer translations by Joachim Neugroschel and Michael Hofmann (see Bibliography).

8. Polgar's essay first appeared in his book *An den Rand geschrieben* (Berlin: Ernst Rowohlt Verlag, 1927).

9. "Selbstveriß," *Werke,* 4: 241.

10. In the opening pages of the novel Roth's narrator remarks casually, yet pointedly, that Frau Bernheim "was, incidentally, of Jewish descent." *Right and Left,* trans. Michael Hofmann (Woodstock, N.Y.: Overlook Press, 1992), 6. However, except for her uneasiness whenever, as often occurs, a guest in her home embarks on a Jewish joke, the family's partly Jewish background plays no role whatever in the lives of its members. Oddly enough, Roth, who knew a Jewish name when he heard one and clearly took pleasure in naming his figures, chose to endow the non-Jewish Herr Bernheim with a surname that is unmistakably Jewish and would have been far more suitable as the maiden name of his wife. It may be that psychologically this misnomer reflects still another of Roth's many attempts to deny the Jewishness of his own father.

11. "Schluß mit der 'Neuen Sachlichkeit,'" *Werke,* 4:246–258.

12. Ibid., 250.

13. *Der stumme Prophet* (Cologne and Berlin: Kiepenheuer and Witsch, 1966); *The Silent Prophet,* trans. David Le Vay (Woodstock, N.Y.: Overlook Press, 1980). The German edition contains an afterword by Werner Lengning that briefly recounts the history of the manuscript, including its editing. An unsigned Publisher's Note at the back of the English translation reproduces Lengning's afterword in a somewhat modified version.

14. *24 deutsche Erzähler* (Berlin: Kiepenheuer, 1929).

15. *Perlefter: Die Geschichte eines Bürgers,* ed. Friedemann Berger (Cologne: Kiepenheuer and Witsch, 1978). In his afterword, Berger provides detailed information on the manuscript—which might more accurately be called a collection of preliminary sketches—that served as the basis for the book.

16. The fragmentary novel *Erdbeeren* (Strawberries) was first published by Roth's

biographer David Bronsen in *Text + Kritik. Sonderband: Joseph Roth,* ed. H. L. Arnold (Munich: Edition Text + Kritik, 1974). It is also contained in *Werke,* 3:193–218.

17. Margarete Willerich-Tocha, *Rezeption als Gedächtnis: Studien zur Wirkung Joseph Roths* (Frankfurt am Main: Peter Lang, 1984), 171–95.

## Chapter 4: The Pinnacle Years, 1930–1932

1. *Job: The Story of a Simple Man,* trans. Dorothy Thompson (Woodstock, N.Y.: Overlook Press, 1982). Further references will follow parenthetically in the text after the abbreviation *J.*

2. The 1648 peasant and Cossack uprising against the Poles in Ukraine, under Bogdan Chmielnicki, led to the greatest Jewish tragedy in Europe prior to the Nazi Holocaust. Amid unspeakable horrors, entire communities were wiped out, a cataclysmic event that was memorialized in the Jewish liturgy through dirges and prayers. See Simon Dubnow, *History of the Jews in Russia and Poland from the Earliest Times to the Present Day,* trans. I. Friedlaender, 3 vols. (Philadelphia: Jewish Publication Society of America, 1916), 1:144–53.

3. See Sidney Rosenfeld, "The Chain of Generations: A Jewish Theme in Joseph Roth's Novels," in *Yearbook 18 of the Leo Baeck Institute,* ed. Robert Weltsch (London: Secker & Warburg, 1973), 227–31. See, too, my discussion of the Bloomfield episode in chapter 2.

4. Ibid., 229.

5. For a critical discussion of this commonly accepted but problematic categorization, with focus on Roth's *Job,* see Sidney Rosenfeld, "Denkmal für eine zerstörte Welt: Joseph Roths *Hiob* und die Frage der deutsch-jüdischen Symbiose, *Tribüne. Zeitschrift zum Verständnis des Judentums* (Frankfurt) 29, no. 116 (1990): 175–185. A shorter, English version, "Joseph Roth's *Hiob* and the Question of [the] German-Jewish Symbiosis," appeared in *Austriaca. Cahiers Universitaires d'Information sur l'Autriche* (Rouen), no. 30 (June 1990): 23–31. Unfortunately, it is marred by many printer's errors.

6. Cited in Bronsen, *Joseph Roth: eine Biographie,* 385. The undated letter is not contained in Roth's collected correspondence.

7. Ibid., 384.

8. For a discussion of the novel's affinities with other works of Jewish ghetto fiction written in German, see Ritchie Robertson, "Roth's *Hiob* and the Traditions of Ghetto Fiction," in *Co-Existent Contradictions: Joseph Roth in Retrospect,* ed. Helen Chambers (Riverside, Calif.: Ariadne Press, 1991), 185–200.

9. Stefan Zweig, *Die Welt von gestern: Erinnerungen eines Europäers* (Stockholm: Bermann-Fischer Verlag, 1944).

10. *Twilight of a World,* trans. H. T. Lowe-Porter (New York: Viking Press, 1937). This book, as such, was published only in translation. The original German version of the prologue later appeared as "Ein Versuch über das Kaisertum Österreich" in the Werfel collection, *Zwischen Oben und Unten,* ed. Adolf D. Klarmann (Munich and Vienna: Langen Müller, 1975), 493–520.

11. Ibid., 40.

12. *Briefwechsel [von] Hugo von Hofmannsthal [und] Josef Redlich,* ed. Helga Fußgänger (Frankfurt: S. Fischer Verlag, 1971), 116.

13. For a discussion of Roth's quest for identity, including his attempt to view himself as a German, see Sidney Rosenfeld, "Joseph Roth and Austria: A Search for Identity," in *Yearbook 31 of the Leo Baeck Institute,* ed. Arnold Pauker (London: Secker & Warburg, 1986), 455–64.

14. *The Radetzky March,* trans. Joachim Neugroschel (Woodstock: Overlook Press, 1995), 161–62. Further references will follow parenthetically in the text after the abbreviation *RM.*

15. After Austrian television showed Michael Kehlmann's two-part film of *The Radetzky March* in 1965, there was criticism from all segments of the public against what was seen as disparagement of the monarchy and its institutions. The most energetic of the protests were directed against the scene in which Franz Joseph was shown standing before a window in his nightshirt and scenes that showed his failing memory. See Otto Breicha, "Empörung gegen den Radetzkymarsch," *Wort in der Zeit* (Vienna), no. 6 (1965): 49.

16. The Marxist literary historian Georg Lukács argued in 1939 that in *The Radetzky March* Roth described only some of the reasons behind Austria's collapse; he showed, said Lukács, how the ruling classes of Austria were no longer able to live in the old way, but then neglected to show that the suppressed classes no longer wanted to live that way. Lukács faulted Roth for depicting this factor, at best, as background to the novel rather than as a decisive factor of the plot. Lukács's article, which appeared in Russian, is translated in its entirety in Fritz Hackert's doctoral dissertation, *Kulturpessimismus und Erzählform: Studien zu Joseph Roths Leben und Werk* (Bern: Herbert Lang, 1967), 147.

17. Franz Werfel, *Der Abituriententag* (Berlin: Paul Zsolnay, 1928), 69–71.

18. Ibid., 71.

19. In a letter dated 24 December 1962, the Prague-born German-language author Johannes Urzidil told me that he had related an anecdote with this same content to Joseph Roth. Urzidil added, however, that since the story was well known at the time, Roth could have gotten it from another source. Without citing Roth's version in *The Radetzky March,* the critic Walter Abendroth—who also got the anecdote from Urzidil—incorporated it into his existential-theological essay, "Reichs- und Bundesvolk: Das zweifache Zeugnis des Joseph Roth," *Hochland* 50, no. 5 (June 1958): 422–429. Abendroth places the entirety of Roth's work in the perspective of a faith covenant shared by Imperial Austria and Orthodox Judaism in like measure.

## Chapter 5: The Exile Years, 1933–1937

1. *Tarabas: A Guest on Earth,* trans. Winifred Katzin (Woodstock, N.Y.: Overlook Press, 1934), 273. Further references will follow parenthetically in the text after the abbreviation *T.*

2. On the precarious situation of the Jews in eastern Europe, see Simon Dubnow,

*History of the Jews in Russia and Poland from the Earliest Times to the Present Day,* trans. I. Friedlaender, 3 vols. (Philadelphia: Jewish Publication Society of America, 1916), 3:66–142.

3. See 1 John 2:18–22.

4. *Antichrist,* trans. Moray Firth (New York: Viking Press, 1935), 91.

5. Ibid., 20. Unfortunately, Roth's translator has omitted Roth's wordplay on the name Hollywood—possibly because it is hard to render effectively.

6. For an informative discussion of the role of the motion picture as a mass medium during the Weimar Republic, see the chapter "Film" in Jost Hermand and Frank Trommler, *Die Kultur der Weimarer Republic* (Munich: Nymphenburger Verlagshandlung, 1978), 261–98. Kracauer's best-known works include his study of class and mass culture, *Die Angestellten* (1930; *The Salaried Masses,* 1998), the film history, written in English, *From Caligari to Hitler: A Psychological History of the German Film* (1947), and his monumental work, *Theory of Film: The Redemption of Physical Reality* (1960).

7. *The Ballad of the Hundred Days,* trans. Moray Firth (New York: Viking Press, 1936), 213. Further references will follow parenthetically in the text after the abbreviation *HD.*

8. A year later, in his foreword to a planned but unrealized reissue of the 1927 essay *The Wandering Jews,* Roth foresaw with despair that for the Jews of Germany there would be no rescue from the militant anti-Semitism there. In the 1975 edition of Roth's works this foreward was appended to the essay; see *Werke,* 3:359–369. Given this all-too-real fear on Roth's part, it is hardly accidental that in physical appearance and destructive intent he likened the fiendish Ramzin in *Tarabas* to Hitler.

9. *Confession of a Murderer: Told in One Night,* trans. Desmond I. Vesey (Woodstock, N.Y.: Overlook Press, 1985), 20. This "footnote" is present in all editions of the novel. Perhaps Roth himself saw the necessity for it, or the publisher urged it on him. In any event, the information it supplies is incomplete. Further references will follow parenthetically in the text after the abbreviation *CM.*

10. For an analysis of Roth's symbolic use of names in the novel, see Sidney Rosenfeld, "Die Magie des Namens in der 'Beichte eines Mörders,'" in *Joseph Roth und die Tradition,* ed. David Bronsen (Darmstadt: Agora Verlag, 1975), 305–17.

11. *Confession of a Murderer,* 217. Most unhappily, the translation skips over the first and symbolically meaningful component of Roth's compound noun *Vogelblicke.* The insertion in the text is mine.

12. *Weights and Measures,* trans. David Le Vay (London: Peter Owen, 1982), 11. Further references will follow parenthetically in the text after the abbreviation *WM.*

13. These observations draw on insights offered by Peter W. Jansen in his unpublished University of Freiburg doctoral dissertation, "Weltbezug und Erzählhaltung: Eine Untersuchung zum Erzählwerk und zur dichterischen Existenz Joseph Roths" (1958), 327.

14. For representative samplings of their pertinent work see, for example, Reinhold Heller, *Brücke: German Expressionist Prints from the Granvil and Marcia Specks*

*Collection* (Evanston, Ill.: The Gallery, 1988); also Otto Nagel, *Käthe Kollwitz* (Dresden: Verlag der Kunst, 1963).

15. Cited in David Bronsen's biography, *Joseph Roth,* 577.

16. Ibid., 577.

## Chapter 6: The Exile Years, 1938–1939

1. This history is documented in Roth's correspondence with the small Catholic publishing house in Bilthoven, Verlag De Gemeenschap: *Aber das Leben marschiert weiter und nimmt uns mit: Der Briefwechsel zwischen Joseph Roth und dem Verlag De Gemeenschap,* ed. Theo Bijvoet and Madeleine Rietra (Cologne: Kiepenheuer and Witsch, 1991). The editors' introduction offers a helpful overview; see pp. 9–29.

2. *The Tale of the 1002nd Night,* trans. Michael Hofmann (New York: St. Martin's Press, 1998), 11. Further references will follow parenthetically in the text after the abbreviation *TN.*

3. In *Der Schwierige* (1921) Hofmannsthal affectionately evoked, in its virtues and failings, the Viennese aristocratic society that faded from the scene with the dissolution of the monarchy. Anatol, a weak and irresponsible amorous adventurer (though not without a measure of melancholy charm), is the central character in Schnitzler's play of 1894 by the same name. Both plays have long since achieved classical status and remain standard works in the Austrian repertory.

4. "Preuße und Österreicher," *Erzählungen und Aufsätze,* vol. 2 of *Augewählte Werke in zwei Bänden* (Frankfurt am Main: S. Fischer Verlag, 1957), 615–17. Hofmannsthal's juxtaposition of the Prussian and Austrian character or mentality was one of several attempts he made during the First World War to define the inspiring ideals of Austrian history. In *Der Schwierige* he reflected these ideals in the figures of Hans Karl Bühl and Helene Altenwyl, whom he placed in opposition to the north German Baron Neuhoff.

5. *Das journalistische Werk 1929–1939,* ed. Klaus Westermann, vol. 3 of *Werke* (Cologne: Kiepenheuer and Witsch, 1991), 544. It must be noted that in comparing Luther with Hitler, Roth's point of departure was not Luther's anti-Judaism; of this, indeed, he was unaware. Rather, he saw in Luther's Reformation the national force that shattered the universalist European tradition founded and nourished by the Catholic Church. More than once in this context, Roth cited the dictum of the Austrian classical dramatist Franz Grillparzer (1791–1872): "Von der Humanität durch Nationalität zur Bestialität" (From humaneness to bestiality as a consequence of nationality).

6. See Bijvoet and Rietra, introduction to *Aber das Leben marschiert weiter,* 17.

7. Ibid., 16–17.

8. *Aber das Leben marschiert weiter,* 153.

9. *The Emperor's Tomb,* trans. John Hoare (Woodstock, N.Y.: Overlook Press, 1984), 156–57. Further references will follow parenthetically in the text after the abbreviation *ET.*

10. Although he does not state it explicitly, Roth clearly implies that this is a

dream his protagonist's father shared with the slain archduke. Indeed, despite his loathing of the Hungarians and lack of sympathy for nearly all of the Slavs, the archduke favored the notion of an Austrian monarchy with power shared alike by Germans, Slavs, and Magyars. C. A. Maccartney stresses, however, that it is "completely untrue that he ever thought of 'remodelling the Monarchy so as to rest it on its Slav elements,' internally any more than in respect of foreign policy." See C. A. Maccartney, *The Habsburg Empire 1790–1918* (New York: The Macmillan Company, 1969), 752–53.

## Chapter 7: Riddles of a Torn Existence

1. In a long quasi-autobiographical letter of 10 June 1930 to his publisher Gustav Kiepenheuer, Roth describes his mother as "a Jewish woman of ample, earthy Slavic build, who often sang Ukrainian songs because she was very unhappy." He continues by noting that his mother was "without money or a husband"—and then disguises the Galician-Jewish identity of his father by calling him "an Austrian of the sly type" (*BR* 165). In this same letter—written well before his exile—Roth states that he has no homeland, that his "fatherland" exists only where things are going badly for him (165).

2. More so than Hofmannsthal, Schnitzler and Altenberg—like the *Volkstück* author Johann Nestroy in the previous century—were representative Viennese writers. Hofmannsthal's cultural significance extends further: he was an *Austrian* writer and within European letters he spoke for Austria's heritage in a way that others of his Viennese contemporaries could not. (In this particular context, the imposing figure and work of Karl Kraus resist categorization.)

3. In the U.S.A. and Europe Bronsen personally interviewed nine persons and corresponded with another two, all of whom had been present at the funeral. See *Joseph Roth: Eine Biographie,* 600–604.

4. It may have attested to Roth's invariably noted charm that three of his onetime lovers came to the burial—besides Andrea Manga Bell, Sybil Rares-Schuster, a Berlin actress, originally from Bukovina, who lived with Roth briefly in Frankfurt in 1929, and the Lithuanian-born Sonja Rosenblum (about whom little seems to be known except that she and Roth were intimately linked). Irmgard Keun was in Holland at the time, but from there she dedicated a deeply felt poem to Roth's memory. In an interview with Bronsen, Andrea Manga Bell testified to Roth's personal magnetism: "Actually, Roth was ugly, but he attracted women strongly, and there were always some who fell in love with him and pursued him. I have never known another man who was sexually so attractive." See *Joseph Roth: Eine Biographie,* 370–71.

5. Joseph Roth , quoted in Bronsen, *Joseph Roth: Eine Biographie,* 198. Bronsen is quoting from "Wiener Symptome," a newspaper article Roth published in *Der Neue Tag* on 22 June 1919.

6. Zweig, too, succumbed to the despair of exile. Mourning the destruction of European culture by Nazism, he and his second wife committed suicide in February 1942 in Brazil.

7. Upon his baptism in 1897, Gustav Mahler (1860–1911) was appointed musical director of the Vienna Court Opera.

8. For a detailed presentation of the conflicting views on Roth's Catholicism, see Bronsen, *Joseph Roth: Eine Biographie,* 488–90. Among those who joined the controversy over Roth's burial, Soma Morgenstern expressed himself most bitterly, even charging the Catholic side with deception. See Soma Morgenstern, *Joseph Roths Flucht und Ende* 274–80, 295–96.

9. Hermann Kesten, "A propos de Joseph Roth," *Allemagne d'aujourd'hui.* 3 (1957):3.

10. Radziwilow—since 1940 Chernovoarmeisk in Ukraine—lay just across the border from Brody in Russian Volhynia. On more than one occasion Roth falsely claimed Volhynia, rather than Galicia, as the region of his birth. By referring specifically to Radziwilow—something he did repeatedly—he perhaps wished obliquely to associate his origins with the noble Polish family of the Radziwils. In any event, here he once again purposefully avoided naming Brody as his birthplace.

11. For a keenly insightful interview with Gottfarstein on Roth's personality, see Bronsen, *Joseph Roth: Eine Biographie,* 543–52. Roth recognized in the younger Gottfarstein, whom he first met in 1936, an authentic, eastern European Jew. During the years of their friendship, Gottfarstein became literally indispensable for him as a conversation partner.

12. Gershom Scholem, *Jews and Judaism in Crisis* (New York: Schocken Books, 1976), 64. Scholem's short polemic may be seen as a prologue to his longer essay on this topic, "Jews and Germans," loc. cit., 71–92.

13. See Theodor Lessing, *Der jüdische Selbsthaß* (Berlin: Jüdischer Verlag, 1930). For an important contemporary study of this syndrome, see Sander L. Gilman, *Jewish Self-Hatred: Anti-Semitism and the Hidden Language of the Jews* (Baltimore: Johns Hopkins University Press, 1986).

14. Less than two years after Weininger's death, his book *Geschlecht und Charakter* (1903; *Sex and Character,* 1906) had been reprinted five times; by 1923 it had seen twenty-five printings. Unlike Weininger, who still commands scholarly interest, Trebitsch has been all but forgotten. The best known among his many books was *Deutscher Geist—oder Judentum! Der Weg der Befreiung* (1921; German Spirit—or Judaism!: The Path to Freedom).

15. Werner Kraft, *Franz Kafka: Durchdringung und Geheimnis* (Frankfurt am Main: Suhrkamp Verlag, 1968), 206.

16. The debate over Kraus's Jewish identity is marked at the one end by the view that he was a Jewish self-hater, and at the other by the view that he was an arch-Jew in the spirit of the prophets. The former is more convincing. See, for example, Nike Wagner, "Inkognito ergo sum: Zur jüdischen Frage bei Karl Kraus," *Literatur und Kritik* (Vienna), no. 219–20 (1987): 387–99.

17. Although I differ with Kraft on the question of Kraus's freedom from anti-Jewish sentiments, in these remarks I have generally followed his exposition. His discussion of Kraus, Kafka, and German-Jewish writers (loc. cit., 199–208) is invaluable for the

depth of its insights and the wide perspectives it opens. On the relationship of Karl Kraus to the thought of Otto Weininger, see Werner Kraft, *Karl Kraus: Beiträge zum Verständnis seines Werke* (Salzburg: Otto Müller Verlag, 1956), 73–94. (In a conversation in Jerusalem in May 1988, Kraft remarked, succinctly and sadly, that Kraus bore a portion of blame for the anti-Semitism that existed within the *Brenner* Circle of Ludwig von Ficker [1880–1967] in Innsbruck. Ficker's nobility of character was beyond question. Possibly, Kraft had the tragic poet Georg Trakl in mind, who was known to harbor ugly Jewish stereotypes.)

18. In his biography, Bronsen speaks forthrightly of Roth's Jewish *self-hate* and of his "occasional strong anti-semitic outbursts" (152–53). He bases this charge on an interview with Roth's lifelong friend from Brody, the physician Eduard Broczyner. Unfortunately, Bronsen did not convey the actual content of the interview.

19. *Das journalistische Werk 1929–1939,* ed. Klaus Westermann, vol. 4 of *Werke* (Cologne: Kiepenheuer and Witsch, 1991), 531. The essay appeared on 30 August 1934 in the Prague journal *Die Wahrheit* and elicited strong rebuttals from Zionist writers in the issue of 22 September 1934; loc. cit., 545.

20. The letter was written on 14 August 1935, three months after the promulgation of the Nuremberg racial laws, which made non-Germans of Jews and thus lent weight to the Zionist argument that the Jewish people required their own homeland. There has been an extensive discussion of Roth's relationship to Zionism. See, for example, David Bronsen, "Joseph Roths lebenslange Auseinandersetzung mit dem Zionismus," *Zeitschrift für die Geschichte der Juden* (Tel Aviv) 7, no. 1 (1970): 1–4; Hansotto Ausserhofer, "Joseph Roth im Widerspruch zum Zionismus," *Emuna-Horizonte* (Frankfurt am Main) 5, no. 5 (1970): 325–330; Matiyahu Kranz, "Joseph Roths Stellung zum Zionismus: Eine Ergänzung zu H. Aussenhofers Aufsatz 'Joseph Roth im Widerspruch zum Zionismus,'" *Tribüne* (Frankfurt am Main) 14, no. 55 (1975): 6376–6392; Mark H. Gelber, "Zur deutsch-zionistischen Rezeptionsgeschichte: Joseph Roth und die *Jüdische Rundschau*," in *Von Franzos zu Canetti: Jüdische Autoren aus Österreich. Neue Studien,* ed. Mark H. Gelber et al. (Tübingen: Max Niemeyer Verlag, 1996), 201–09.

21. Léon Blum (1872–1950) became premier when the coalition Popular Front, which he headed, won the French elections in 1936. In December 1946, he served briefly as interim premier.

22. For an instructive overview that aims to revise the commonly held notion of blanket rejection and even hatred of the refugees by the Jews of Germany, see Jack Wertheimer, "'The Unwanted Element': East European Jews in Imperial Germany," in *Yearbook 26 of the Leo Baeck Institute,* ed. Arnold Pauker (London: Secker & Warburg, 1981), 23–46. Wertheimer's findings also generally apply to Austria.

23. See Arnold Zweig and Hermann Struck, *Das ostjüdische Antlitz* (1919) and Alfred Döblin, *Reise in Polen* (1921; *Journey to Poland,* 1991). In addition to Roth's *Juden auf Wanderschaft,* these were two major works among others by German writers that treated the everyday culture of the *Ostjuden.* For an informative introduction to the subject, see Michael Brenner, "The Invention of the Authentic Jew: German-Jewish

Literature," in *The Renaissance of Jewish Culture in Weimar Germany* (New Haven and London: Yale University Press, 1996), 129–52.

24. Kafka's fascination with east European Jewry was decisively stimulated by his friendship in Prague with the Polish-born Yiddish actor Jizchak Löwy. It is copiously documented in his diary entries of the years 1911–1912.

25. Although I have arrived at these thoughts independently, I wish to acknowledge the primacy of David Bronsen and my debt to him for information and insight. In more compact form than in his indispensable Roth biography, Bronsen searches out both the sociohistorical and the elusive inner determinants of Roth's personality in his article "The Jew in Search of a Fatherland: The Relationship of Joseph Roth to the Habsburg Monarchy," *The Germanic Review* 54, no. 2 (spring 1979): 54–61.

26. Katharina Ochse suggests that in *The Wandering Jews* as well as in *Job* Roth deliberately hid his Catholic sympathies because he wished to be regarded publically as a Jewish writer. This suggests, in turn, that Roth was moved by material considerations, i.e., he wished to avoid alienating both potential Jewish reviewers and buyers of the two books. If he indeed calculated in this way, it casts his ethical character in a disturbing light. See Katharina L. Ochse, "'1922 France = la lumière, la liberté PERSONELLE, (pas une phrase!).' Joseph Roths Reise durch Frankreich 1925," in *Joseph Roth. Der Sieg über die Zeit: Londoner Symposium,* ed. Alexander Stillmark (Stuttgart: Verlag Hans-Dieter Heinz, 1996), 174.

27. Bronsen, loc. cit., 54.

28. Alfred Polgar, *Taschenspiegel,* ed. Ulrich Weinzierl (Vienna: Löcker Verlag, 1979), 72–73.

# Selected Bibliography

## Works by Joseph Roth

German Editions

*Collected Works*

*Werke in drei Bänden.* 3 vols. Ed. by Hermann Kesten. Cologne and Berlin: Kiepenheuer and Witsch, 1956.

*Werke: Neue erweiterte Ausgabe in vier Bänden.* 4 vols. Ed. Hermann Kesten. Cologne: Kiepenheuer and Witsch, 1975–76.

*Werke.* 6 vols. Vols. 1–3, *Das journalistische Werk,* edited by Klaus Westermann. Cologne: Kiepenheuer and Witsch, 1989–90. Vols. 4–6, *Romane und Erzählungen,* edited by Fritz Hackert. Cologne: Kiepenheuer and Witsch, 1989–91.

*Individual Works*

*Hotel Savoy.* Berlin: Verlag Die Schmiede, 1924.

*Die Rebellion.* Berlin: Verlag Die Schmiede, 1924.

*Juden auf Wanderschaft.* Berlin: Verlag Die Schmiede, 1927.

*Die Flucht ohne Ende.* Munich: Kurt Wolff Verlag, 1927.

*Zipper und sein Vater.* Munich: Kurt Wolff, 1928.

*Rechts und Links.* Berlin: Gustav Kiepenheuer Verlag, 1929.

*Hiob: Die Geschichte eines einfachen Mannes.* Berlin: Gustav Kiepenheuer, 1930.

*Radetzkymarsch.* Berlin: Gustav Kiepenheuer, 1932.

*Tarabas: Ein Gast auf dieser Erde.* Amsterdam: Querido, 1934.

*Der Antichrist.* Amsterdam: Allert de Lange, 1934.

*Beichte eines Mörders, erzählt in einer Nacht.* Amsterdam: Allert de Lange, 1936.

*Die hundert Tage.* Amsterdam: Allert de Lange, 1936.

*Das falsche Gewicht: Die Geschichte eines Eichmeisters.* Amsterdam: Querido Verlag, 1937.

*Die Kapuzinergruft.* Bilthoven: De Gemeenschap, 1938.

*Die Geschichte von der 1002: Nacht.* Bilthoven: De Gemeenschap, 1939.

*Die Legende vom Heiligen Trinker.* Amsterdam: Allert de Lange, 1939.

*Der stumme Prophet.* Cologne and Berlin: Kiepenheuer and Witsch, 1966.

*Das Spinnennetz.* Cologne and Berlin: Kiepenheuer and Witsch, 1967.

*Briefe 1911–1939.* Cologne and Berlin: Kiepenheuer and Witsch, 1970.

*Der Neue Tag: Unbekannte politische Arbeiten 1919–1927. Wien, Berlin, Moskau.* Cologne and Berlin: Kiepenheuer and Witsch, 1970.

*Perlefter: Die Geschichte eines Bürgers: Fragment eines Romans aus dem Berliner Nachlaß.* Cologne: Kiepenheuer and Witsch, 1978.

*Berliner Saisonbericht: Unbekannte Reportagen und journalistische Arbeiten 1920–1939.* Cologne: Kiepenheuer and Witsch, 1984.

*Aber das Leben marschiert weiter und nimmt uns mit: Der Briefwechsel zwischen Joseph Roth und dem Verlag De Gemeenschap.* Cologne: Kiepenheuer and Witsch, 1991.

*Unter dem Bülowbogen: Prosa zur Zeit.* Cologne: Kiepenheuer and Witsch, 1994.

## English Editions

*Antichrist.* Trans. Moray Firth. New York: Viking Press, 1935.

*The Ballad of the Hundred Days.* Trans. Moray Firth. New York: Viking Press, 1936.

*Flight without End.* Trans. David Le Vay and Beatrice Musgrave. Woodstock, N.Y.: Overlook Press, 1977.

*The Silent Prophet.* Trans. David Le Vay. Woodstock, N.Y.: Overlook Press, 1980.

*Job: The Story of a Simple Man.* Trans. Dorothy Thompson. Woodstock, N.Y.: Overlook Press, 1982.

*Weights and Measures.* Trans. David Le Vay. London: Owen, 1982.

*The Emperor's Tomb.* Trans. John Hoare. Woodstock, N.Y.: Overlook Press, 1984.

*Confession of a Murderer: Told in One Night.* Trans. Desmond I. Vesey. Woodstock, N.Y.: Overlook Press, 1985.

*Hotel Savoy: Fallmerayer the Stationmaster: The Bust of the Emperor.* Trans. John Hoare. Woodstock, N.Y.: Overlook Press, 1986.

*Tarabas: A Guest on Earth.* Trans. Winifred Katzin. Woodstock, N.Y.: Overlook Press, 1987.

*The Spider's Web.* Trans. John Hoare. London: Chatto and Windus, 1988.

*Zipper and His Father: The Spider's Web.* Trans. John Hoare. Woodstock, N.Y.: Overlook Press, 1989.

*Right and Left: The Legend of the Holy Drinker.* Trans. Michael Hofmann. Woodstock, N.Y.: Overlook Press, 1992.

*The Radetzky March.* Trans. Joachim Neugroschel. Woodstock, N.Y.: Overlook Press, 1995.

*The Tale of the 1002nd Night.* Trans. Michael Hofmann. New York: Saint Martin's Press, 1998.

*Rebellion.* Trans. Michael Hofmann. New York: St. Martin's Press, 1999.

*The Wandering Jews.* Trans. Michael Hofmann. New York: W. W. Norton, 2000.

## Critical Works

*Selected Books*

Arnold, Heinz Ludwig, ed. *Joseph Roth.* Munich: Edition Text + Kritik, 1982. Most notable for the first printing of Roth's twenty-page "Romanfragment" *Erdbeeren* (Strawberries), a planned but never completed autobiographical novel. An accompanying article by David Bronsen elucidates its history and significance within Roth's work.

Bronsen, David. *Joseph Roth: Eine Biographie.* Cologne: Kiepenheuer and Witsch, 1974. In addition to archival and related work on three continents, Bronsen conducted 160 interviews in twelve countries and fifty cities with relatives, friends, and acquaintances of Roth, perhaps all of them now deceased. Bronsen's biography is definitive; it cannot be superceded.

———. *Joseph Roth: Eine Biographie.* Kiepenheuer and Witsch, 1993. An abridgment by Katarina Ochse, with selected bibliography by Rainer-Joachim Siegle.

———, ed. *Joseph Roth und die Tradition: Aufsatz- und Materialiensammlung.* Darmstadt: Agora Verlag, 1975. A valuable collection of original and reprinted reminiscences and biographical and interpretative essays. A standard reference source.

Chambers, Helen, ed. *Co-Existent Contradictions: Joseph Roth in Retrospect.* Riverside, Calif.: Ariadne Press, 1989. Eleven papers presented at the 1989 Leeds University commemorative symposium. The three sections deal respectively with Roth's literary reception, his journalism, and his fiction. Especially noteworthy is the editor's contribution, "Predators or Victims: Women in Joseph Roth's Work"; also Ritchie Robertson, "Roth's *Hiob* and the Traditions of Ghetto Fiction."

Cziffra, Géza von. *Der heilige Trinker: Erinnerungen an Joseph Roth.* Bergisch-Gladbach: Bastei-Lübbe, 1983. An anecdotal memoir of encounters with Roth.

Kessler, Michael and Fritz Hackert, eds. *Joseph Roth: Interpretation- Kritik- Rezeption. Akten des internationalen, interdisziplinären Symposions 1989, Akademie der Diözese Rottenberg-Stuttgart.* Tübingen: Stauffenberg Verlag, 1990. A weighty volume rich with substantial contributions by an international roster of Roth scholars and critics. The articles cover a broad spectrum of themes.

Koester, Rudolf. *Joseph Roth.* Berlin: Colloquium Verlag, 1982. A concise, informative, and lucidly presented introduction to Roth's life and major works, which draws judiciously on the secondary literature. An excellent starting point for further acquaintanceship with Roth.

Lunzer, Heinz and Viktoria Lunzer-Talos. *Joseph Roth: Leben und Werk in Bildern.* Cologne: Kiepenheuer and Witsch, 1994. A splendidly executed photo documentation with gracefully composed commentary and excerpts from Roth's journalistic work. Many of the photos published here for the first time. Useful and pleasurable to read.

Magris, Claudio. *Weit von wo: Verlorene Welt des Ostjudentums,* Trans. Jutta Prasse. Vienna: Europa Verlag, 1974. The subtitle of the original 1971 Italian edition makes clear what this wide-ranging, deep-delving study is about: "Joseph Roth and the East European Jewish Tradition." Practically a history of Yiddish literature and American-Jewish writing as the context for exhaustively detailed literary interpretations of Roth's work. Magris's likewise detailed psychoanalytic elucidations lead to less persuasive results.

Marchand, Wolf R. *Joseph Roth und völkisch-nationalistische Wertbegriffe: Untersuchungen zur politisch-weltanschaulichen Entwicklung Roths und ihrer Auswirkung auf sein Werk.* Bonn: Bouvier, 1974. Traces the development of Roth's political views from his early "socialist" involvement to the pronounced conservatism of his later years. Marchand extracts unconvincing connections to fascist ideology from *The Radetzky March* and *The Ballad of the Hundred Days.*

Morgenstern, Soma. *Joseph Roths Flucht und Ende. Erinnerungen.* Lüneburg: zu Klampen, 1994. An intimate memoir of Morgenstern's lifelong friendship with Roth, starting with their youth. Especially valuable for its depiction of Roth's last years, his decline, and his death. The long-past conversations with Roth are probably more dependable for their content than for their word-for-word accuracy. Along with Bronsen, an indispensable biographical source.

Müller-Funk, Wolfgang. *Joseph Roth.* Munich: Verlag C. H. Beck, 1989. A thematically structured study that views Roth's work in a broadly delineated cultural-historical context while seeking to construct an inner biography. The results are original and stimulating.

Nürnberger, Helmuth. *Joseph Roth in Selbstzeugnissen und Bilddokumenten.* Reinbek: Rowohlt, 1981. An illustrated overview of Roth's life and work in the traditional format of the *rowohlts monographien* series. A handy introduction although its content is derivative.

Scheible, Hartmut. *Joseph Roth: Mit einem Essay über Gustav Flaubert.* Stuttgart: Kohlhammer, 1971. Contains detailed interpretations of *Zipper and His Father, The Radetzky March,* and *The Emperor's Tomb.* Bothersome for its overly polemical tone, but otherwise an insightful study of Roth's novels based on close analysis of their language and stressing a "loss of reality" as the most salient aspect of their content.

Siegel, Rainer-Joachim. *Joseph Roth-Bibliographie.* Morsum: Cicero Presse, 1995. A painstakingly comprehensive and detailed bibliography of Roth's publications and the secondary material. Numerous faulty references and omissions, which will hopefully be corrected in a new edition. Nonetheless, a milestone in Roth research.

Steinmann, Esther. *Von der Würde des Unscheinbaren: Sinnerfahrung bei Joseph Roth.* Tübingen: Niemeyer, 1984. A literary-critical / theological analysis of religious experience and cognition in *Job, The Radetzky March, The Ballad of the Hundred Days, Confession of a Murderer,* and *The Legend of the Holy Drinker.* Steinmann's analysis clarifies the religious impulse behind the Napoleon novel (though it makes the book no better). A highly concentrated, demanding study.

Stillmark, Alexander, ed. *Joseph Roth: Der Sieg über die Zeit: Londoner Symposium.* Stuttgart: Verlag Hans-Dieter Heinz, 1996. Eleven papers on the occasion of Roth's hundredth birthday. Of special interest among several articles of high quality: A. Stillmark's analysis of *Confession of a Murderer* and its affinities to Dostoyevsky and K. Ochse's discussion of Roth's 1925 travel series from southern France and its significance for his Catholic inclinations.

Sültemeyer, Ingeborg. *Das Frühwerk Joseph Roths 1915–1926: Studien und Texte.* Vienna and Freiburg: Herder, 1976. A study of Roth's early work, with special attention to his political development. Based on the journalistic texts discovered by Sültemeyer, above all "Reise in Rußland," and later published by her with extensive commentary as *Der Neue Tag* (see list of Individual Works). The argument that Roth's socialism was genuine is overdone.

Westermann, Klaus. *Joseph Roth, Journalist: Eine Karriere, 1915–1939.* Bonn: Bouvier, 1987. An exhaustive pioneer study of Roth's career as a journalist. Also contains an important section on Roth's changing relationship toward the Habsburg monarchy. Lucidly written and highly informative. Should be regarded as a standard sourcework.

Willerich-Tocha, Margarete. *Rezeption als Gedächtnis. Studien zur Wirkung Joseph Roths.* Frankfurt am Main: Peter Lang, 1984. An unusually stimulating study of Roth's literary production and its reception from the start of his career to the mid-1980s. Covers varied venues of reception, from literary and academic criticism to school curricula and criticism of Roth's filmed novels. Extensive bibliography, including Roth translations and films.

*Selected Articles*

Abendroth, Friedrich. "Reichs- und Bundesvolk: Das zweifache Zeugnis des Joseph Roth." In *Joseph Roth und die Tradition,* ed. David Bronsen, 87–97. Darmstadt: Agora Verlag, 1975. Further references to this source will be referred to as Bronsen. Emphasizes the religious affinities between Judaism and Austrianism as the constituitive elements of Roth's work. Opens avenues of understanding.

Böhm, Anton. "Das große schwarze Gesetz. Notizen zu Joseph Roths Gesamtwerk." *Wort und Wahrheit* (Vienna) 14, no. 5 (1959): 345–58. In his broad characterization of Roth's work and person, Böhm focuses on the author as Austrian, Jew, and cultural German. Many stimulating insights.

Böll, Heinrich. "Die Trauer, die recht behielt: Leben und Werk von Joseph Roth." *Deutsche Rundschau* 83, no. 3 (March 1957): 274–278. A brief but instructive essay on Roth's life and work. An early assessment, like the two above, and can be read with much profit by readers seeking a gateway to adequately understanding Roth.

Bronsen, David. "The Jew in Search of a Fatherland: The Relationship of Joseph Roth to the Habsburg Monarchy." *The Germanic Review* 54 (Spring 1979): 54–61. Probably the most revealing attempt to probe the workings of Roth's inner conflict between Jewish and Austrian identity. Highly recommended.

Butler, G. P. G. "Radetzky Limp." *German Life and Letters* 29, no. 3 (April 1976): 388–393. A witty, trenchant critique of Eva Tucker's 1974 "retranslation" of Geoffrey Dunlop's 1933 English version of *The Radetzky March.* Readers without German will be alerted by Butler to the fact that, in general, Roth has been ill-served by more than just two of his older translators into English.

Dohrn, Verena. "Verfallen wie in Brody: Joseph Roth und Isaak Babel: Schriftsteller im Grenzland." *Die Neue Rundschau* 101, no. 2 (1990): 53–62. Vividly captures the atmosphere of Brody and Galicia as settings for Roth's work. Incorporated as "Verfallen wie in Brody" in Dohrn's book *Reise nach Galizien: Grenzlandschaften des alten Europa* (Frankfurt am Main: S. Fischer, 1991).

Forst de Battaglia, Otto. "Joseph Roth: Wanderer zwischen drei Welten." In Bronsen, 77–86. Insightful depiction of Roth as a writer hopelessly in search of a home between the shtetl of Brody, the imperial city of Vienna, and the City of Lights, Paris. An early commentary still well worth reading.

Gordimer, Nadine. "The Empire of Joseph Roth." *New York Review of Books,* 5 December 1991, 16–19. A perceptive appreciatory essay on Roth's literary universe by a writer of international stature. Although Gordimer describes the east European Jewish component of Roth's work, she oddly neglects his major novel *Job.*

Grubel, Fred. "Mein Vetter Muniu." In *Sie flohen vor dem Hakenkreuz: Selbstzeugnisse der Emigranten: Ein Lesebuch für Deutsche,* ed. Walter Zadek and Christine Brinck, 229–35. Reinbek: Rowohlt, 1991. Personal recollections of Roth by his Leipzig maternal cousin (later executive director of the Leo Baeck Institute in New York, which houses the largest Roth archive).

Hackert, Fritz. "Kaddisch und Miserere: Untergangsweisen eines jüdischen Katholiken. Joseph Roth im Exil." In *Die deutsche Exilliteratur, 1933–1945,* ed. Manfred Durzak, 220–31. Stuttgart: Reclam, 1973. A substantial, tightly woven discussion of Roth's Jewish and Catholic dichotomies: without having converted, Roth harbored a Catholic view of life.

———. "Joseph Roth: *Radetzkymarsch.*" In *Deutsche Romane des 20: Jahrhunderts: Neue Interpretationen,* ed. Paul Michael Lützeler, 183–99. A thought-provoking view of the historical and political "mythologies" of Roth's novel in the context of the "crisis of the historical novel" during the Weimar period.

Horch, Hans Otto. "'Im Grunde ist er sehr jüdisch geblieben . . .': Zum Verhältnis von 'Katholizismus' und Judentum bei Joseph Roth." In *Literatur in der Gesellschaft: Festschrift für Theo Buck zum 60: Geburtstag,* ed. Frank-Ruther Hausmann et al., 211–24. Tübingen: Narr, 1990. A substantial contribution to the ongoing dispute over Roth's "Jewish Catholicism." The title of the article, taken from a contemporary personal remark on Roth ("At bottom he has remained very Jewish"), indicates the thrust of Horch's stimulating article. The question of how a professing Catholic can remain basically Jewish also finds no resolution here.

Howes, Geoffrey C. "Joseph Roth's *Kapuzinergruft* as a Document of 1938." In *Austrian Writers and the Anschluss: Understanding the Past—Overcoming the Past,* ed. Donald G. Daviau, 156–67. Riverside, Calif.: Ariadne Press, 1991. Shows how the willful ignorance of Roth's protagonist contributes to Austria's political misfortune. Underscores the historical disjuncture with *The Radetzky March.*

Hüppauf, Bernd. "Joseph Roth: Hiob: Der Mythos des Skeptikers." In *Im Zeichen Hiobs: Jüdische Schriftsteller und deutsche Literatur im 20: Jahrhundert,* ed. Gunter E. Grimm and Hans-Peter Bayersdörfer, 309–25. Königstein: Athenäum, 1985. Portrays *Job* as marking a turn toward philosophical skepticism in Roth's career. Sees Roth's later conservatism and reactionary view of history as outgrowths of this skepticism. As a heuristic approach, the thesis proves too narrow.

Kerekes, Gabor. "Der Teufel hieß Jenö Lakatos aus Budapest: Joseph Roth und die Ungarn." *Literatur und Kritik,* no. 243–44 (April–May 1990): 157–69. Examines Roth's Hungarian prejudices and shows them to have been real.

Lardner, Susan. "An Enemy of His Time." *The New Yorker,* 23 November 1987, 154–60. A somewhat impressionistic, but sensitive, overview of Roth's life and work. Flawed by biographical inaccuracies, but thanks to its insights, a nice supplement to both Gordimer and Miron.

118

Miron, Susan. "On Joseph Roth." *Salmagundi,* no. 98–99 (spring–summer 1993): 198–206. A sketchy overview with large omissions by a nonspecialist, but insightful. A helpful starting point for non-readers of German.

Müller, Klaus-Detlef. "Joseph Roth: Radetzkymarsch. Ein historischer Roman." In *Interpretationen: Romane des 20: Jahrhunderts, Band 1,* 298–321. Stuttgart: Reclam, 1993. Defines the structural limitations and the literary accomplishment of *The Radetzky March* as a historical novel. Reveals perceptively how the forces of illusion, decadence, and decline that determine Austria's end are mirrored in the story of the Trottas.

Peter, Klaus. "Die Stummheit des Propheten: Zu Joseph Roths nachgelassenem Roman." In *Basis: Jahrbuch für deutsche Gegenwartsliteratur, 1,* ed. Reinhold Grimm and Jost Hermand, 153–167. Frankfurt: Athenäum, 1970. Treats Roth's posthumous novel, *The Silent Prophet,* its political content, and the problems posed by its incomplete form.

Reich-Ranicki, Marcel. "Joseph Roths Flucht ins Märchen." *Nachprüfung: Aufsätze über deutsche Schriftsteller von gestern,* 202–28. Munich: Piper, 1977. A literary appreciation by a sensitive reader and master critic. A perceptive, stimulating portrait.

Rosenfeld, Sidney. "Joseph Roth and Austria: A Search for Identity." *Publications of the Leo Baeck Institute: Year Book 31,* ed. Arnold Paucker, 455–64. London: Secker & Warburg, 1986. Examines Roth's existential homelessness and his lifelong search for a rooted identity between Brody, Vienna, Berlin, and Paris.

Schwarz, Egon. "Joseph Roth und die österreichische Literatur." In Bronsen, 131–152. A sociohistorical discussion with paradigmatic results. Schwarz tackles the thorny question of an Austrian national literature and defines the place of Roth's work—as that of a German-Jewish writer from Galicia—within it and within the larger context of European social and cultural history.

Shaked, Gershom. "Wie jüdisch ist ein jüdisch-deutscher Roman?: Über Joseph Roths *Hiob.*" In *Juden in der deutschen Literatur: Ein deutsch-israelisches Symposion,* ed. Stéphan Moses and Albrecht Schöne, 281–292. Frankfurt am Main: Suhrkamp, 1986. A semiotic analysis of *Job,* which aims to set criteria for defining the Jewish character of a "German-Jewish" novel. The problem is irresolvable, but Shaked furthers our understanding of it by pointing out the role of Yiddish as a key aspect of the novel's cultural code.

Spiel, Hilde. "Eine Welt voller Enkel." In *Romane von gestern—heute gelesen: Band 2, 1918–1933,* ed. Marcel Reich-Ranicki, 350–358. Frankfurt am Main: S. Fischer Verlag, 1989. Adds nothing new to the many perceptive commentaries on *The Radetzky March* long since available, yet thanks to Spiel's warm, graceful prose—a tribute from one Austrian writer to another—a happy reading experience (and an enlightening one, too).

Williams, Cedric E. "Joseph Roth: A Time out of Joint." *The Broken Eagle: The Politics of Austrian Literature from Empire to Anschluss,* 91–112. New York: Barnes and Noble Books, 1974. One of the most astute general articles on Roth in English. Rock solid, critical, and full of stimulating ideas.

# Index

Page numbers in bold type denote extended discussion of Roth's works.

Abendroth, Walter, 105n. 19
*Abituriententag, Der* (Class Reunion;
    Werfel), 48–49
"Against the Myth of the German-Jewish
    Dialogue" (Scholem), 90
Albania, 27
alcohol use: by Roth, 13, 14, 43, 74, 89;
    in Roth's works, 14–15, 49, 50, 72
Aleichem, Sholem, 44
Alexandrovna, Natasha (character), 29
Alja (character), 29
Altenberg, Peter, 87, 108n. 2
alter egos, 63
American P.E.N. Club, 14
"Amerikanismus im Literaturbetrieb,
    Der" (Americanism in the Literary
    Market; Roth), 102–3n. 3
*Anatol* (Schnitzler), 76, 107n. 3
Anschluss, 13, 48, 74, 81, 82, 85, 87.
    *See also* Austria
*Antichrist, Der* (Roth), 14, 62–63, 92,
    93, 95
Antichrist figure, 62–63, 66
"anti-fiction" narrative technique, 36
anti-Semitism, 9, 13, 18, 27, 34, 46, 62,
    91–92, 93, 106n. 8, 110n. 17. *See
    also* Jews
appearance versus reality, 46–47
*Arabian Nights,* 75
*Arbeiter-Zeitung,* 16
Arnold, Herr (character), 24
assimilation, 12, 44, 46, 67, 95, 96
Association for the Protection of German
    Writers, 88

atonement. *See* sin and repentance
Auerbach, Berthold, 11
Austria: and Anschluss, 13, 48, 74, 81,
    82, 85, 87; borders of, after World
    War I, 52; in "Bust of the Emperor,"
    3–4, 5, 55; Dollfuss as ruler of, 45; in
    *Emperor's Tomb,* 13, 47, 80–86; First
    Republic of, 10, 85, 88–89, 97; in
    *Flight without End,* 29–30; Habsburg
    Austria, 4, 5–8, 10, 14, 45–48,
    52–55, 75–80, 82–83, 85, 89, 97,
    99n. 7; Hitler in, 9; Jews of, 7–9,
    21–22, 46, 87–89; Musil on, 7; Nazi
    party in, 86; in *Radetzky March,* 5,
    13, 45–55, 80, 82–84, 97, 105n. 16;
    in *Rebellion,* 23–25; Roth on his love
    for, 45; shah's 1873 visit to Vienna,
    75; in *Silent Prophet,* 36; in *Tale of
    the 1002nd Night,* 13, 74–80; in
    *Weights and Measures,* 13, 70–73; in
    World War II, 14
Austrian universality, 3–4, 47, 83, 89
autobiographical or pseudo-autobio-
    graphical elements, 27–28, 67

*Ballad of the Hundred Days, The* (Roth),
    **63–66,** 67, 74, 97
Bartels, Adolf, 11
Battaglia, Otto Forst de, 45
*Beichte eines Mörders, erzählt in einer
    Nacht* (Roth). *See Confession of a
    Murderer* (Roth)
Benjamin, Walter, 11, 96
Berger, Friedemann, 103n. 15

*Berlin Alexanderplatz* (Döblin), 28
*Berliner Abend-Zeitung,* 13
*Berliner Börsen-Courier,* 16
Bernheim, Frau (character), 103n. 10
Bernheim, Herr (character), 103n. 10
Bernheim, Paul (character), 27–28,
   33–35, 39
Bernheim, Theodor (character), 34–35
Bible, 39, 99–100n. 9. *See also* Job motif
Bidak, Leo (character), 37
Bismarck, Otto von, 79
Bloomfield, Henry (character), 21–22
Blum, Léon, 93, 110n. 21
Blumenfeld, Jechiel (character), 21
Blumich, Katharina (character), 24, 25
Böhlaug, Alexander (character), 21
Böhlaug, Phöbus (character), 21
Böll, H., xii
Bolshevik Revolution, 27, 36, 56–57
Book-of-the-Month Club, 39
bourgeoisie: in *Perlefter: The Story of a
   Bourgeois,* 36–38; in *Right and Left,*
   33–35; in *Zipper and His Father,* 31
Branco, Joseph (character), 84–85
Brandeis, Nikolai (character), 22, 34–35
Brecht, Bertolt, 12
*Brenner* Circle, 110n. 17
Brentano, Bernard von, 11
Brock, 33
Broczyner, Eduard, 110n. 18
Brody, Austria, xv, 4–6, 9, 12, 22, 28, 44,
   67, 71, 87–88, 94, 100n. 11, 109n.
   10, 110n. 18
Bronsen, David, xi, xii, 88, 95–96, 100n. 10,
   104n. 16, 108nn. 3–4, 110n. 18, 111n. 25
Buber, Martin, 22, 41, 54, 96
*Buch der Lieder* (Heine), 11
Bühl, Count Kari (character), 76, 107n. 4
Burger, Heinz Otto, 2
"Bust of the Emperor, The" (Roth), 3–4,
   5, 55
"Büste des Kaisers, Die" (Roth). *See*
   "Bust of the Emperor, The" (Roth)

Catholicism, 14, 26, 53, 55, 62, 63,
   88–90, 92, 95, 107n. 5, 108–9n. 8,
   111n. 26
"chain of generations," 21–22, 41
Chmielnicki massacres, 40, 104n. 2
Chojnicki, Count (character), 47, 51, 54,
   83–85
*Christliche Ständestaat, Der,* 14
chronology of Roth's life and works,
   xv–xvii
clown symbol, 33
coffee houses, 30–32, 81, 86
Communists, 14, 19, 36, 62, 88
*Confession of a Murderer* (Roth), **66–70,**
   97, 106n. 9, 106n. 11
continuity and transience, 56–62. *See
   also* generational bond
Csokor, Franz Theodor, 45

Dan, Gabriel (character), 19–22, 27–28
De Gemeenschap, 80, 81
Demant, Max (character), 49, 51–55, 92
Döblin, Alfred, 17, 18–19, 28, 94, 101n.
   2, 110n. 23
documentary style, 28–33, 35
Dollfuss, Engelbert, 45
Dos Passos, John, 103n. 3
Dostoyevsky, Fyodor, 60

Ehrenburg, Ilya, 73
Eibenschütz, Anselm (character), 71–73
*Emperor's Tomb, The* (Roth), 4, 13, 47,
   74, **80–86,** 87, 92, 97
Enders, Carl (character), 34
Enders, Irmgard (character), 34
*Erdbeeren* (Strawberries; Roth), 103–4n. 16
*Erfolg* (Feuchtwanger), 101n. 2
"Es lebe der Dichter" (Long Live the
   Poet: Roth), 29, 35
Eustachius (character), 61
evil and goodness, 56–62, 67–70
expatriates, 102n. 3
eyewitness author-narrator, 29–33

*Fabian* (Kaestner), 28
*Fackel, Die,* 102n. 6
Fallada, Hans, 28
*Falsche Gewicht, Das* (Roth). *See Weights and Measures* (Roth)
father-son relationship: in *Emperor's Tomb,* 82, 107n. 10; in *Radetzky's March,* 47–54; of Roth, 28, 87, 92, 96, 103n. 10, 108n. 1; in *Tarabas,* 60–61; in *Zipper and His Father,* 30–33
Feuchtwanger, Lion, 18, 101n. 2
Ficker, Ludwig von, 110n. 17
film industry, 62–63
first-person narrative, 81
Fitzgerald, F. Scott, 28, 102n. 3
*Flight without End* (Roth), 17, 20, **26–30,** 36, 56
*Flucht ohne Ende, Die. See Flight without End* (Roth)
Forst de Battaglia, O., xii
framework narrator, 70
France: in *Confession of a Murderer,* 67–70; in *Flight without End,* 30; and Napoleon, 63–66; Popular Front in, 110n. 21; Roth's death in, 16; Roth's funeral in, 88–89; Roth's travel reports from, 26
*Frankfurter Zeitung,* 10–11, 13, 19, 26–27, 29, 45, 102–3n. 3
Franz Joseph, Emperor, 8, 47–48, 52–55, 76–77, 80, 81, 85, 89, 97, 105n. 15
Franzos, Emil, 44
Frederick II, 79
Freudian interpretation, 96

G., Madame (character), 30
gambling, 50
generational bond: "chain of generations" and Jews, 21–22, 41; severed generational bond in *Radetzky March,* 47–52, 66. *See also* father-son relationship

Germany: conflict of German-Jewish identity, 11–12, 90–96; in *Flight without End,* 29, 30; Nazism in, 1, 2, 12, 13, 16, 17, 37, 45, 46, 66, 81, 97, 106n. 8; travel report by Roth on, 27; Vatican's 1933 Concordat with Nazi Germany, 62; Weimar Republic of, 10, 13, 16–17, 19, 20, 28, 34; writers from, 11–12
*Geschichte von der 1002. Nacht, Die* (Roth). *See Tale of the 1002nd Night* (Roth)
Gidon, Blanche, 63, 65, 93
*Gilgi, eine von uns* (Keun), 100n. 15
Glaeser, E., 28
God: as Great Weights Inspector, 72–73; and Napoleon's destiny, 63–66; rebellion against, 24–25, 39–44, 72
Golubchik, Semyon (character), 67–70, 73
Gottfarstein, Joseph, 90, 109n. 11
Great Weights Inspector, 72–73
Grillparzer, Franz, 107n. 5
Grübel, Jechiel, 21–22
Grübel, Paula, 9
guilt, 60–62, 67, 70, 73

Habsburg, Otto von, 55, 88
Habsburg Austria, 4, 5–8, 10, 14, 45–48, 52–55, 75–80, 82–83, 85, 89, 97, 99n. 7. *See also* Austria
Hackert, Fritz, 100n. 11
Hartmann, Irene (character), 30
heathenry, 23–24
Heckel, Erich, 72
*Heimat* (rootedness in national and cultural identity), 12
Heine, Heinrich, 11, 89, 90
Hemingway, Ernest, 28, 102n. 3
Herzl, Theodor, 9–10
*Hiob* (Roth). *See Job* (*Hiob;* Roth)
Hitler, Adolf, 1, 9, 12, 13, 14, 17, 18, 45, 46, 66, 79, 81, 89, 106n. 8, 107n. 5
Hofmann, Michael, 103n. 7

Hofmannsthal, Hugo von, 3, 46, 76, 99n. 7, 107nn. 3–4, 108n. 2
Hollywood film industry, 62–63, 106n. 5
*Hotel Savoy* (Roth), 11, 17, **19–23**, 27, 37
house imagery, 31–32, 69, 86
hubris and fall, 67
humor, 75. *See also* irony
*Hundert Tage, Die* (Roth). *See Ballad of the Hundred Days, The* (Roth)

Ignatz (character), 20
"Im mittäglichen Frankreich" (In the South of France; Roth), 26
injustice, 23–25
irony, 15, 23–25, 52, 70, 75, 89
Italy, 27

Jadlowker (character), 71, 72
Jansen, Peter W., 106n. 13
Jelacich, *rittmaster* (character), 50
Jews: anti-Semitism against, 9, 13, 27, 34, 46, 62, 91–92, 93, 106n. 8, 110n. 17; of Austria, 7–9, 21–22, 46, 87–89; and "chain of generations," 21–22, 41; and Chmielnicki massacres, 40, 104n. 2; conflict of German-Jewish identity, 11–12, 90–96; in *Emperor's Tomb,* 84–85, 86, 92; in *Flight without End,* 27–28; homelessness of, 4, 7–9, 12, 92, 93; in *Hotel Savoy,* 21; in *Job,* 23, 39–45, 53, 55, 92, 95; and *kaddish,* 41; *Ostjude* (east European Jew), 4, 5, 9, 10, 27, 44, 54–55, 56, 62, 85, 90, 93–96, 110n. 23; in *Perlefter: The Story of a Bourgeois,* 37; pogrom against, 59–60; in *Radetzky March,* 49, 52, 54–55, 92; in *Right and Left,* 22, 34, 103n. 10; Roth's Jewish identity, 4–5, 12, 53, 67, 87–90, 92–93, 95–96, 103n. 10, 108n. 1, 109n. 16, 110n. 18; self-

hatred of, 91–92; and shtetl literature, 44; in *Spider's Web,* 17–19; in *Tarabas,* 56–62, 92; in *Weights and Measures,* 71; in western Europe, 93–94; and Yom Kippur, 42, 95; and Zionism, 6, 9–10, 87, 91–96, 110nn. 19–20
*Job* (*Hiob;* Roth), xi, 1, 2, 13, 23, 38, **39–44**, 45, 53–55, 64, 65, 71, 75, 92, 95, 97, 111n. 26
Job motif: in *Ballad of the Hundred Days,* 64; in *Job,* 39–45, 55; in *Rebellion,* 25
John, Gospel of, 99–100n. 9
journalistic writings, 10–11, 13, 14, 16, 17, 19, 26–27, 29, 34, 35, 62, 108n. 5
*Juden auf Wanderschaft* (The Wandering Jews; Roth), 9, 27, 62, 93–95, 106n. 8, 110n. 23, 111n. 26
*Judenstaat, Der* (Jewish State; Herzl), 10
*Jüdisches Lehrhaus,* 22
justness and evil, 56–62

*kaddish,* 41
Kaestner, Erich, 28
Kafka, Franz, 91, 109n. 17, 110–11n. 24
Kaleguropulos (character), 20
Kalergi, Lt. Col. (character), 79
"Kapitel Revolution, Ein" (A Chapter from the Revolution; Roth), 36
Kapturak (character), 50, 71
*Kapuzinergruft, Die (The Emperor's Tomb;* Roth), 4, 13
Kargan, Friedrich (character), 35–36
Kartak, Andreas (character), 14–15
Kästner, E., 28
Kayser, Wolfgang, xi
Kehlmann, Michael, 105n. 15
Kesten, Hermann, xi, xii, 1, 2–3, 5, 28, 36, 90
Keun, Irmgard, xii, 6, 100n. 15, 108n. 4
Kiepenheuer, Gustav, 43, 108n. 1

*Kind aller Länder* (Keun), 100n. 15
Kio (character), 48–49
Kisch, Egon Erwin, 1, 88
*Kleiner Mann-was nun* (Fallada), 28
Klein-Haparash, Jakob, 8
Kollwitz, Kathë, 72
Komrower (character), 70
Kracauer, Siegfried, 10–11, 63
Kraft, Werner, 91, 109–10n. 17
Krapotkin, Prince (character), 68
Krapotkin, Princess (character), 68
Krapotkin, Sergei (character), 68, 69, 70
Kraus, Karl, xi, 91, 102n. 6, 108n. 2,
      109–10n. 17
Kreutzer, Magdalene (character), 78, 79
Kristianpoller, Nathan (character),
      56–60, 62

Lakatos, Jenö (character), 68
Landau, Max, 6
Lazik (character), 78
League for Austrian Culture, 88
*Legende vom heiligen Trinker, Die* (The
      Legend of the Holy Drinker; Roth),
      14–15
Lengning, Werner, 103n. 13
Lenz, Benjamin (character), 18, 19
Lenz, Lazar (character), 18
Leo Baeck Institute, 36
Lessing, Theodor, 91
Liebknecht, Karl, 16
Liga für das Geistige Österreich (League
      for Austrian Culture), 88
Lissauer (character), 77
*Literarische Welt,* 34
Lock (character), 33
Lohse, Theodor (character), 17–19, 20,
      28, 34
"lost generation" after World War I, 28,
      102n. 3
Löwy, Jizchak, 111n. 24
Lueger, Karl, 9

Lukács, Georg, 105n. 16
Lutetia (character), 69–70
Luther, Martin, 79, 107n. 5
Luxemburg, Rosa, 16

Maccartney, C. A., 108n. 10
Magris, Claudio, 99n. 7
Mahler, Gustav, 89, 108n. 7
*Man without Qualities, The* (Musil), 45
Manga Bell, Andrea, 66, 108n. 4
Mann, Heinrich, 1, 17
Mann, Thomas, 12
*Mann ohne Eigenschaften, Der* (Musil),
      7
Maria (character), 61
Martini, Fritz, 2
*Maskenspieler* (dissembler or player of
      divers roles), 5, 10
Matzner, Josephine (character), 76, 77,
      78, 79
*Mein Kampf* (Hitler), 9
*Mein Weg als Deutscher und Jude* (My
      Life as German and Jew; Wasser-
      mann), 90
messianism, 92
Morgenstern, Soma, 100n. 10, 100n. 14,
      109n. 8
Morstin, Count Franz Xaver (character),
      3–4, 5, 99–100n. 9
mourning, 41
Musil, Robert, 7, 45

*Nach Mitternacht* (Keun), 100n. 15
Napoleon, 63–66
narrative techniques: "anti-fiction" nar-
      rative technique, 36; eyewitness
      author-narrator, 29–33; first-person
      narrative, 81; frame structure and
      flashback episodes, 75; framework
      narrator, 70; in later novels, 74–75
National-Socialism. *See* Nazism
nationalism, 47, 83, 88, 93, 107n. 5

Nazism: as Antichrist, 62; and Austria, 48, 55, 74, 81; in Germany, 1, 2, 12, 13–14, 16, 17, 37, 45, 46, 62, 66; Roth's opposition to, 88, 89, 97; in *Spider's Web,* 17–19, 20; Vatican's 1933 Concordat with Nazi Germany, 62; and Zionism, 93

Nestroy, Johann, 108n. 2

*Neue Rundschau,* 36

*Neue Sachlichkeit. See* New Objectivism

*Neue Tag, Der,* 10, 108n. 5

*Neue Tage-Buch, Das,* 14

Neugroschel, Joachim, 103n. 7

New Objectivism, 28–29, 30, 32, 33, 35, 36, 37, 39, 41

newspapers. *See* journalistic writings; and specific newspapers

Nikitsch, Euphemia (character), 71, 72

Nolde, Emil, 72

Nowak (character), 71

Ochse, Katharina, 111n. 26

Onufrij (character), 71

order and rebellion, 56–62

*Österreichische Post, Die,* 14, 97, 102n. 6

*Ostjude* (east European Jew), 4, 5, 9, 10, 27, 44, 54–56, 62, 85, 90, 93–96, 110n. 23

P., Eduard (character), 30–31, 32, 33

Pansin, Zwonimir (character), 22

*Pardon wird nicht gegeben* (Döblin), 101n. 2

*Pariser Tageszeitung,* 14

Percoli, Tino (character), 80, 97

Peretz, Isaac Leib, 44

Perlefter, Alexander (character), 37

*Perlefter: The Story of a Bourgeois* (Roth), **36–38**, 103n. 15

Petri, Angela (character), 64

Pichenik, Nissen (character), 57, 62, 71

Piniowsky, Solomon (character), 55

pogrom, 59–60

Poland, 1, 6, 12, 20, 27, 40, 94

Polgar, Alfred, 32, 97, 103n. 8

post–World War I period: in *Flight without End,* 28–30; in *Hotel Savoy,* 19–23; "lost generation" in, 28, 102n. 3; in *Rebellion,* 23–25; in *Right and Left,* 33–35; in *Zipper and His Father,* 30–33

*Prager Tagblatt,* 16

"Preuße und Österreicher" (Prussian and Austrian; Hofmannsthal), 76, 107n. 4

prostitution, 49, 76, 77–78, 79

Prussia, 76, 79, 81, 107n. 4

Pum, Andreas (character), 23–25, 39, 72, 102n. 6

*Radetzky March* (film), 105n. 15

*Radetzky March* (Roth), xi, 1, 2, 4, 5, 13, **45–55**, 64–66, 75, 79, 80, 82–84, 86, 89, 92, 97, 105n. 16

Radziwil family, 109n. 10

Ramzin (character), 59–60, 106n. 8

Rares-Schuster, Sybil, 108n. 4

Rathenau, Walther, 13, 16–17, 34

rebellion and order, 24–25, 56–62

*Rebellion, Die* (Roth), 17, 19, **23–25**, 37, 39, 72

*Rechts und Links* (Roth). *See Right and Left* (Roth)

Redlich, Josef, 46

Reformation, 107n. 5

Reichler, Friederike, 10, 37, 43, 53, 66, 73, 74

Reifenberg, Benno, 26

Reinthaler, Heinrich, 102n. 6

"Reise in Rußland" (Russian Journey; Roth), 11

Reisiger, Manes (character), 84–85, 92

repentance. *See* sin and repentance

Rifkin, Channa Lea (character), 70

*Right and Left* (Roth), 17, 27, **33–35**, 103n. 10

*Romane, Erzählungen, Aufsätze* (Roth), 3
Roosevelt, Eleanor, 14
Rosenblum, Sonja, 108n. 4
Rosenzweig, Franz, 96
Roth, Maria, 6, 87, 94, 96
Russia. *See* Soviet Union
Russian Revolution, 27, 36, 56–57

Sameschkin (character), 71
*Saturday Review of Literature,* 39
Savelli (character), 36
Schickele, René, 11, 37, 66
Schinagl, Mizzi (character), 75–80
schizophrenia, 37, 53
"Schluß mit der 'Neuen Sachlichkeit'!"
    (Enough of "Neue Sachlichkeit"!;
    Roth), 35
Schmidt-Rotluff, Karl, 72
Schnitzler, Arthur, 76, 87, 107n. 3, 108n. 2
Scholem, Gershom, 90, 109n. 12
Schuschnigg, ex-Chancellor, 14
Schutzverband Deutscher Schriftsteller
    (Association for the Protection of
    German Writers), 88
Schwarzschild, Leopold, 14
*Schwierige, Der* (Hofmannsthal), 76,
    107nn. 3–4
Seelig, Carl, 60
"Segen des ewigen Juden, Der" (The
    Blessing of the Wandering Jew;
    Roth), 92
"Selbstverriß" (Panning Myself; Roth),
    34, 35
Sforim, Mendele Mokher, 44
shadows, 63
shah (character), 75–80
Shemariah (character), 57, 60, 61, 92
shtetl literature, 44
Siberia, 29, 85. *See also* Soviet Union
Sieburg, Friedrich, 11
*Silent Prophet, The* (Roth), **35–36**, 103n. 13
sin and repentance, 60–65, 67–70, 72–73
Singer, Deborah (character), 41, 42, 43

Singer, Jonas (character), 40, 42, 44
Singer, Mendel (character), xi, 39–44,
    55, 71, 92
Singer, Menuchim (character), 40–42,
    43, 44
Singer, Miriam (character), 40, 42, 43,
    44
Singer, Sam (Shemariah) (character), 40,
    44
Skowronnek, Dr. (character), 52
Slama (character), 71
Socialists and socialism, 11, 14, 16, 19, 93
Sonnemann, Leopold, 10
Soviet Union: in *Antichrist,* 62; collapse
    of, 8; in *Confession of a Murderer,*
    67–70; in *Flight without End,* 29; in
    *Job,* 39–41; Roth's travel report on,
    27, 62; and Russian Revolution, 27,
    36, 56–57; in *Silent Prophet,* 35–36;
    Stalin in, 36; success of *Hotel Savoy*
    in, 11; in *Tarabas,* 56; Trotsky in, 36
*Spider's Web, The* (Roth), 11, **16–19**, 20,
    28, 34
*Spinnennetz, Das* (Roth). *See Spider's
    Web, The* (Roth)
Staiger, Emil, xi
Stalin, Joseph, 36
*Strawberries* (Roth). *See Erdbeeren*
    (Strawberries; Roth)
Struck, Hermann, 110n. 23
*Stumme Prophet, Der* (Roth). *See Silent
    Prophet, The* (Roth)
subjectivity, 35, 39–44
*Sun Also Rises, The* (Hemingway), 102n. 3
Szwaby/Schwabendorf, 5, 71, 100n. 11

Taittinger, Baron Alois Franz von (charac-
    ter), 75–80
*Tale of the 1002nd Night, The* (Roth), 13,
    **74–80**, 89, 97
*Tarabas: A Guest on Earth* (Roth), **56–62**,
    67, 92, 97, 106n. 8
Tarabas, Nicholas (character), 56–62, 67, 73

*Tender Is the Night* (Fitzgerald), 102n. 3
themes. *See* specific themes
Thérèse de Lisieux, Sainte, 15
Third Reich. *See* Nazism
Thompson, Dorothy, 14, 39
*3. November 1918* (Csokor), 45
Toller, Ernst, 1, 15, 17, 89
Trakl, Georg, 110n. 17
transience and continuity, 56–62
translations of Roth's works, 11, 39, 63,
    103n. 7, 106n. 5, 106n. 11
travel reports, 26–27
Trebitsch, Arthur, 91, 109n.14
Trotsky, Leon, 36
Trotta, Carl Joseph von (character), 47–53,
    71, 79, 80, 81, 82, 84
Trotta, Elizabeth (character), 81
Trotta, Franz Ferdinand (character), 80–87
Trotta's father (character), 48, 49, 50–51, 53
Trotta's grandfather (character), 47, 48,
    49–50, 52–54, 81
Trummer, Ignaz (character), 78, 79
Tucholsky, K., 28
Tunda, Franz (character), 20, 27, 28,
    29–30, 39, 56
Tunda, George (character), 30
*Twilight of a World* (Werfel), 45–46, 104n. 10

United States: in *Job,* 40–41, 44; Roth's
    refusal to move to, 14; in *Tarabas,* 56–57
Untermeyer, Louis, 39
Urzidil, Johannes, 105n. 19

*Vorwärts,* 19

W., Countess (character), 76, 79

*Wahrheit, Die,* 110n. 19
Wassermann, Jakob, 11, 90
"Weißen Städte, Die" (The White Cities;
    Roth), 26
*Weights and Measures* (Roth), 13, 67,
    **70–73,** 74, 97
Weimar Republic, 10, 13, 16–17, 19, 20, 28,
    34. *See also* Germany
Weininger, Otto, 91, 109n.14
Weizmann, Chaim, 92
Werfel, Franz, 45–46, 48–49, 104n. 10
*Werke* (Roth), 3, 26, 104n. 16
*Werke in drei Bänden* (Roth), 3
"Wiener Symptome" (Roth), 108n. 5
Wilder, Erna (character), 32–33
Wilhelm, Emperor, 79
Willi (character), 25
World War I and World War I veterans, 10,
    27–28, 45, 51–53, 57, 67, 86, 94, 107n.
    4. *See also* post–World War I period

Xandl (character), 78

Yiddish, 6, 41, 44
Yom Kippur, 42, 95

Zionism, 6, 9–10, 87, 91–96, 110nn. 19–20
Zipper, Arnold (character), 30–33, 39, 82
Zipper, Caesar (character), 31
Zipper (father) (character), 30–33, 36
*Zipper and His Father* (Roth), 17, 27,
    **30–33,** 36
Zlotogrod (character), 72
Zweig, Arnold, 94, 110n. 23
Zweig, Stefan, 1, 13, 45, 46, 62, 66–67, 74,
    89, 90, 92, 93, 108n. 6